MOODY
GOLD

MOODY GOLD

COMPILED BY RAY COMFORT

**BRIDGE
LOGOS
FOUNDATION**

Alachua, Florida 32615

Bridge-Logos
Alachua, FL 32615 USA

Moody Gold
by Ray Comfort

Copyright ©2009 by Bridge-Logos

All rights reserved. Under International Copyright Law, no part of this publication may be reproduced, stored, or transmitted by any means—electronic, mechanical, photographic (photocopy), recording, or otherwise—without written permission from the Publisher.

Printed in the United States of America.

Library of Congress Catalog Card Number: 2009929180
International Standard Book Number 978-0-88270-962-8

Unless otherwise indicated, Scripture quotations are from the *Holy Bible: King James Version.*

G163.316.N.m906.35230

My sincere thanks to
Trisha Ramos
for her editorial research.

Contents

Biography of Dwight L. Moody 1

Illustration Portfolio 31

Moody Gold 51

Dwight Lyman Moody
1837-1899

A Brief History

Dwight Lyman Moody was born on Feb. 5, 1837, in Northfield, Massachusetts. At the age of 17 he went to Boston and entered the retail boot and shoe trade with his uncle. While in Boston he came in contact with evangelical Protestant Christians, chiefly through the Young Men's Christian Association (YMCA) and a local Congregational church. In 1856, he moved to Chicago to enhance his business opportunities, where he also deepened his spiritual commitments. He soon became a leader in these circles, chiefly through his work for the local YMCA.

In 1860 Moody abandoned his business career to work full time for the YMCA. He served as president of the Chicago branch from 1865 to 1868. He also ran a large independent Sunday school for slum families, which was supported chiefly by local members of the YMCA. This experience was essential in preparing him for his eventual calling as an evangelist.
In 1867 Moody visited England and immediately established contacts with significant English evangelists. In 1872 he launched his formal career as an evangelist in Great Britain, accompanied by Ira D. Sankey, his famous singing partner

in all his subsequent major meetings. They first attracted widespread popular support in Scotland; then they moved south into England for a long series of campaigns, climaxed by a 4-month visit in London in 1875.

That year Moody returned to the United States as a national figure and immediately launched a series of revival campaigns. While preaching in New York, Philadelphia, Chicago, and Boston, he created the basic structure of urban mass evangelism that is still used by many such ministries today. It was chiefly a feat of organization which sought to adapt the traditional theological and institutional practices of the evangelical movement to the new urban environment created by industrialism.

Although Moody never abandoned his work as an evangelist, after 1880 his vocation expanded. He founded three schools: two private secondary academies in Northfield, Massachusetts, and the Chicago (later renamed Moody) Bible Institute, a training school for urban lay evangelists. He aided national officials of the YMCA in inaugurating the Student Volunteer movement in 1886—a major expression of the evangelical missionary impulse. At the Northfield schools he also held numerous summer adult and youth conferences offering informal Christian education.

Theologically conservative, Moody was dismayed by the rapidly changing intellectual climate of the late 19th century. He found it difficult to deal effectively with the splits between liberals and conservatives in the American churches. His career as an evangelist had noticeably declined by the time he died in December 1899.

Emma Revell Moody (D.L. Moody's wife)

Born in London in 1842, her family immigrated to Chicago in 1849 when she was only seven. After graduating from high school, she taught briefly, and on August 28, 1862 she married Moody. The Lord blessed them with several children—a daughter, Emma Reynolds Moody, and two sons, William Revell And Paul Dwight Moody. Emma served with her husband in Sunday school work, evangelistic campaigns, and took care of much of his correspondence. She died in 1903.

D.L. Moody's Early life

D.L. Moody was of old New England Puritan stock. For seven generations, or two hundred years, his ancestors lived the quiet lives of farmers in the Connecticut Valley. Moody inherited the vigorous constitution and hardy common sense of the typical New Englander. He was the sixth child in a family of nine children, and was born in 1837, in the town of Northfield, Massachusetts. His home town was always very dear to him, and it was one of the greatest pleasures of his life to return to it after a long and arduous evangelistic campaign.

Moody's father, a small farmer and stone mason, was an alcoholic and died at the early age of forty-one, when Moody was only four years old. He left his widow (who was pregnant with Moody's twin brother and sister) in poverty with a mortgage on the home and seven children to support. The creditors seized everything they could, even to the firewood, and the children had to stay in bed until school time to keep warm. A brother of the widowed mother then came to their rescue and helped to relieve their immediate needs. In their extremity Rev. Mr. Everett, the Unitarian minister, was very kind to them, and all the Moody children became members of his Sunday school, and were enlisted as workers to bring in other children.

It was here, therefore, that young Moody began his successful career as a Sunday school worker. Moody's mother had sought to bring up her children as a Christian mother should and Moody never wandered into gross sins as so many young men have done. Lying, complaining, breaking promises, or talking evil about others, was never allowed in the home. One evening when the children had little to eat, they divided their scant supply with a beggar. When Moody was eight years of age, he and an elder brother were crossing the river in a skiff with a boatman who was too drunk to row the boat, and who would not let them touch the oars. They were drifting with the current, but Moody urged his brother to trust in the Lord, and they came safely to land. Moody was mischievous but not wicked as a boy. The Moody family was so poor that the boys would carry their shoes and stockings in their hands on their way to church, to save them from wear, and when in sight of the church would put them on. Moody thought it hard, after working all week, to have to go to church and listen to a sermon he did not understand. In one instance, the preacher had to send someone to the gallery to awaken him. But he got in such a habit of going that he could not stay away, and he afterwards said that he thanked his mother for making him go when he did not feel like going.

At ten years of age, Moody left home in company with another brother to work at a place about thirteen miles away. This nearly broke his mother's heart, as she had striven so hard to keep the family together. He was fondly attached to his mother and sorrowed over leaving her. When he arrived at the new place an aged man gave him a penny and bade him trust the Lord. "That old man's blessing has followed me for fifty years," said Moody. While working there, he received cornmeal porridge and milk, three times a day. He complained to his mother, but when she found out that he had all he wanted to eat, she sent him back. Even during this time, she continued to send them to church. His oldest brother ran away and was not heard from by the family until many years later.

Moody didn't attend school beyond the fifth grade; he couldn't spell, and his grammar was awful. His manners were often brash and crude, and he never became an ordained minister. Once, before his conversion, he so outraged an Italian shoe salesmen with a prank, that the man chased him with a sharp knife, clearly intending to kill him. Yet, Dwight L. Moody was used by God to lead thousands of people to Christ.

This is the wonderful thing about the life of D. L. Moody. Spurgeon was eloquent. George Whitefield was brilliant. John Wesley was also brilliant. Moody is someone you and I can not only identify with, but take strong consolation from the fact that God can use anyone for His purposes. In fact, it seems from Scripture that God passes over the eloquent and the brilliant and uses shepherd boys from nowhere to fulfill His purposes. — Ray Comfort

At seventeen years of age, Moody, tired of farm life and ambitious to work his way upward in the world, decided to go to Boston. He arrived there without any money, and tried in vain to find work until he was almost in despair and felt all alone in the big city. His uncle took him on as a shoe salesman—on condition that he be obedient and that he attend Mt. Vernon Congregational Church where Dr. Edward Norris Kirk was pastor. He succeeded well as a salesman, and over the next eleven months, Moody listened to sermon after sermon from Kirk. The church itself had been formed twelve years earlier by Bostonians unhappy with the rigid doctrinal exclusiveness of another large city church. Pastor Kirk emphasized the sinfulness of man and man's inability to save himself. He spoke of Christ's death on the Cross for all mankind, of Christ's resurrection from the dead, and of

Christ's desire to be the friend of each one who trusted Him. On the other hand, the minister issued dire warnings to all who refused so great a salvation, and he verbally assaulted those who failed to do so.

The biblical way to convince any sinner of his inability to save himself is to put him up the river Niagara, without a paddle. Reveal the holiness of God and the sinfulness of man by preaching the moral Law. Show that God sees the thought life, considers lust to be adultery (Matthew 5:27-28) and hatred to be murder. – Ray Comfort

Moody's upbringing in the Unitarian church taught him that Christ was not fully divine and did not emphasize human need for salvation from sins. Now, listening to Kirk, Moody heard about those things. Having but little schooling, he took but little part in the discussions in the class in Sunday school, but gradually became deeply interested in the study of the Bible, and finally took part in the discussions in the class. Pastor Kirk's messages and his Sunday school teacher Edward Kimball's teaching combined in Moody's mind, and he found himself caught up in a spiritual struggle. But he decided that he wanted to enjoy the pleasures of the world and wait to get saved until just before he died.

This is the attitude of most young men, but thanks to God and to the tenacious attitude of Edward Kimball, life didn't go the way Moody intended. May we be tenacious with the lost. We should only give up on someone when they stop breathing. No sooner. – Ray Comfort

Repeatedly stressing that the spiritual issue was one of choice and of yielding one's will to Another, Kirk emphasized that this choice led to a life of faith. Young Moody sensed the minister was right, yet seemed unable to yield his will to God.

However, the kindness of Kimball, turned young Moody into his life-long friend, and encouraged him to persist in his church attendance and regular Bible reading. Though Moody did try to read the Bible, he couldn't understand it. Kimball later stated, "I can truly say, and in saying it I magnify the infinite grace of God as bestowed upon him, that I have seen few persons whose minds were spiritually darker than was his when he came into my Sunday School class; and I think that the committee of the Mount Vernon Church seldom met an applicant for membership more unlikely ever to become a Christian of clear and decided views of Gospel truth, still less to fill any extended sphere of public usefulness."

Then in April, Mount Vernon Church held a meeting. And on Saturday, April 21, 1855, Edward Kimball resolutely decided to speak to his recalcitrant Sunday school pupil about his soul. Kimball came to the shoe store to ask Moody to commit his life to Christ. Arriving at the store, he found that Moody was in the back, wrapping shoes. He didn't want to embarrass him, however, and almost had decided to come back at a more convenient time. "I began to wonder whether I ought to go just then during business hours," he later reported. And I thought maybe my mission might embarrass the boy, that when I went away the other clerks might ask who I was, and when they learned might taunt Moody and ask if I was trying to make a good boy out of him. Then, I decided to make a dash for it and have it over at once."

Going over to Moody in the back of the shoe store, "I placed my hand on his shoulder, leaned over, and placed my foot on a shoe box." Kimball looked into Moody's eyes and "asked him to come to Christ, who loved him and who wanted his love and should have it." Moody's struggle came to a head, and he surrendered his will to God's will and came to Christ through Kimball's invitation.

"My plea was a very weak one," Kimball observed later, "but I was sincere." He also realized, "The young man was just ready for the light that broke upon him. For there, at once, in the back of that shoe store in Boston, Dwight gave himself and his life to Christ."

The following morning as he left his room, Moody's joy knew no bounds. The wide grin on his face and the fresh sparkle in his big brown eyes reflected his newfound life in Christ. He sensed, "The old sun shone a good deal brighter then it ever had before—I felt that it was just smiling upon me; and as I walked out upon Boston Common and heard the birds singing in the trees, I thought they were all singing a song to me." As he marched along, it seemed all creation cheered him on his way, and he sensed that "I had not a bitter feeling against any man, and I was ready to take all men to heart" (Harvey, *Moody* 28-30).

It is often the way of God to open the heavens with a new convert, but then he is lead into the wilderness to be tempted by the Devil. When I became a Christian I had never known joy like it. But then I went into a wilderness experience and had never known depression like it. The heat of the sun sure did make me send me roots down deep, and I have to say, "It was good for me that I was afflicted, that I might learn your statutes." — Ray Comfort

Moody's whole life was now changed, and became one of joyful Christian service. "Before my conversion," says he, "I worked towards the Cross, but since then I have worked from the Cross; then I worked to be saved, now I work because I am saved." Immediately he began sharing his faith with others, including his own family. They wanted nothing to do with his faith. "I will always be a Unitarian," his mother said. (However, she converted shortly before her death.)

Moody was now running over with zeal and love for the Master, but he did not seem to have received much help and encouragement from the conservative deacons and church members in the church which he was attending. In May 1855, he was denied church membership, because he was "not sufficiently instructed in Christian doctrine." Three of the committee who examined him were appointed to instruct him in the way of God more perfectly. When asked what Christ had done for him, the nervous boy replied that he wasn't aware of anything particular. Leaders felt that was an unacceptable answer, and he was not received as a church member until May 4, 1856.

Chicago and the Civil War

In September 1856, Moody moved to Chicago, where he united with the Plymouth Congregational Church and became a very active Christian worker, putting his soul and energy into the work of winning men to Christ. He found a little mission Sunday school in Chicago where they had sixteen teachers and only twelve scholars. Here he applied to become a teacher. They consented on condition that he would find his own scholars. This just suited his taste, and the next Sunday he arrived with eighteen little hoodlums which he had gathered from the streets. He soon had the building crowded. The great meeting awakened by Finney spread to Chicago, and Moody was in his element. Meanwhile he was prospering in his business, and was so good a salesman of shoes that his employer sent him out as a commercial traveler.

In the spring of 1857, he began to minister to the welfare of the sailors in Chicago's port, then gamblers and thieves in the saloons. He had a passion for saving souls and determined never to let a day pass without telling someone the gospel of Jesus Christ. Often he irritated strangers on the street by asking them if they were Christians—but his pointed questioning stirred the consciences of many. God would use the converted shoe salesman to become the leading evangelist of his day.

A contemporary witness recalls these days

"The first meeting I ever saw him at was in a little old shanty that had been abandoned by a saloon-keeper. Mr. Moody had got the place to hold the meetings in at night. I went there a little late; and the first thing I saw was a man standing up with a few tallow candles around him, holding a negro boy, and trying to read to him the story of the Prodigal Son and a great many words he could not read out, and had to skip. I thought, 'If the Lord can ever use such an instrument as that for His honor and glory, it will astonish me.'"

His work led to the largest Sunday school of his time. As a result of his tireless labor, within a year the average attendance at his school was 650, while 60 volunteers from various churches served as teachers. In the fall of 1858, he began another mission school on a larger scale in another part of the city. The large hall was soon overcrowded. He then procured a larger hall, which afterward developed into one of the leading churches of Chicago. This big hall he soon had filled with street "gamins." The children loved him and crowded in by the hundreds and sang the hymns with great enjoyment. Moody also enticed them in with prizes, free pony rides, picnics, candies, and other things dear to the hearts of children. Scholars were allowed to transfer to any class they desired by simply notifying the superintendent; and this plan resulted in the survival of the fittest teachers. The school soon numbered 1,500. Moody decided to build a church and issued certificates on the "North Market Sabbath School Association; capital $10,000; 40,000 shares at 25 cents each." The Sunday school grew to such proportions that parents were drawn in, and then meetings were held almost every night in the week.

Many prominent men assisted Moody in the Sunday school and in the meetings, but so much devolved on him that he had sometimes to be both janitor and superintendent. This practical training contributed much to his success as a preacher. Doubtless he needed such training, as at first he seemed to have spoken very awkwardly in public. When he first arose to speak in a prayer-meeting one of the deacons assured him that, in his opinion, he would serve God best by keeping still. Another critic, who praised Moody for his zeal in filling the pews at Plymouth Church, said that he should realize his limitations and not attempt to speak in public. "You make too many mistakes in grammar," said he. "I know I make mistakes," was the reply, "and I lack many things, but I'm doing the best I can with what I've got." He then paused, and looking at the man searchingly, inquired, in his own inimitable way, "Look, here, friend, you've got grammar enough—what are you doing with it for the Master?"

Mr. Moody's great Sunday school work was accomplished before he was more than twenty-three years of age. With all his work for Christ he had no thought of entering the ministry until he found that souls were being led to Christ through his efforts. He then decided to give up the business in which he had been engaged, and in which he had already made over $7,000, and devoted all his time to Christian work.

The growing Sunday school congregation needed a permanent home, so Moody started a church, the Illinois Street Church. It became so well known that the just-elected President Lincoln visited and spoke at a Sunday school meeting on November 25, 1860.

After the Civil War began in 1861, Moody was involved with the U.S. Christian Commission of the YMCA and paid nine visits to the battle-front, holding meetings and distributing gospels and tracts among the soldiers and prisoners of war quartered in Chicago and on many leading battlefields of the Southern States. He was present among the Union soldiers after the conflicts of Shiloh, Pittsburgh Landing, and Murfreesboro, and ultimately entered Richmond with the army of General Grant.

After the war, he returned to Chicago and again devoted himself to Sunday school and YMCA work. His Sunday school was so great a success that it made him famous all over the country. Inquiries concerning his methods of work came from all directions, and people traveled thousands of miles to learn them. He was called to many places to address Sunday school conventions and to help organize Sunday school work. Through his efforts, many Sunday schools were led to agree to use the same lessons each Sunday, and thus the International Sunday School lessons were started.

In 1867 Mr. Moody made up his mind to go to Great Britain and study the methods of Christian work employed in that country. He did so, accompanied by Mrs. Moody, who was suffering from asthma. He was particularly anxious to hear Spurgeon, the great English preacher, and George Muller, who had the large orphanages at Bristol. Moody was then unknown in England except to a few prominent Sunday school leaders, but he spoke a number of times in London and Bristol with good results.

It was during this first visit to Britain that Moody heard the words which set him hungering and thirsting after a deeper Christian experience and which marked a new era in his life. The words were spoken to him by Mr. Henry Varley, the well known evangelist, as they sat together on a seat in a public park in Dublin. The words were these: "The world has yet to see what God will do with and for and through and in and by the man who is fully consecrated to Him."

"He said *a man*," thought Moody, "he did not say a *great* man, nor a *learned* man, nor a *smart* man, but simply *a man*. I am a man, and it lies with the man himself whether he will or will not make that entire and full consecration. I will try my utmost to be that man."

The words kept ringing in his mind, and burning their way into his soul until finally he was led into the deeper, richer, fuller experience for which his soul yearned. The impression the words made was deepened soon afterward by words spoken by Mr. Bewley, of Dublin, Ireland, to whom he was introduced by a friend.

"Is this young man all O and O?" asked Mr. Bewley. "What do you mean by 'O and O'?" said the friend. "Is he out and out for Christ?" was the reply. From that time forward Moody's desire to be "O and O" for Christ was supreme.

Moody returned home, and his hunger for a deeper spiritual experience was deepened by the preaching of Henry Moorehouse, the famous English boy preacher, who visited Moody's church in Chicago soon after Moody returned to the United States. For seven nights Moorehouse preached from the text, John 3:16, "For God so loved the world, that he gave his only begotten Son, that whosoever believeth in him should not perish, but have everlasting life." Every night he rose to a higher and higher plain of thought, beginning at Genesis and going through the Bible to Revelation, showing how much God loved the world. He pointed out how God loved the world so much that He sent patriarchs and prophets, and other holy men to plead with the people, and then He sent His only Son, and when they had killed Him, He sent the Holy Ghost.

In closing the seventh sermon from the text, he said: "My friends, for a whole week I have been trying to tell you how much God loves you, but I cannot do it with this poor stammering tongue. If I could borrow Jacob's ladder and climb up into Heaven and ask Gabriel, who stands in the presence of the Almighty, to tell me how much love the Father has for the world, all he could say would be, 'God so loved the world, that he gave his only begotten Son, that whosoever believeth in him should not perish, but have everlasting life.'"

Moody's heart melted within him as he listened to the young preacher describing the love of God for lost mankind. It gave him such a vision of the love of God as he had never seen before, and from that time forward Moody's preaching was of a more deeply spiritual character.

Moody had become one of the most prominent YMCA workers in the United States, and it was at a YMCA convention in Indianapolis, Indiana, in 1870, that he first met Ira David Sankey, who was destined to become his great singing partner. Moody was so impressed with his singing that he asked him to come with him and sing for him, and in Indianapolis they held their first meeting together, in the open air. Some months afterward, Sankey gave up his business and joined Mr. Moody in his work.

Moody continued to hunger for a deepening of his own spiritual life and experience. He had been greatly used of God, but felt that there were much greater things in store for him. The year 1871 was a critical one with him. He realized more and more how little he was fitted by personal acquirements for his work, and how much he needed to be qualified for service by the Holy Spirit's power.

This realization was deepened by conversations he had with two ladies who sat on the front pew in his church. He could see by the expressions on their faces that they were praying. At the close of the service they would say to him, "We have been praying for you."

"Why don't you pray for the people?" Mr. Moody would ask.

"Because you need the power of the Spirit," was the reply.

"I need the power! Why," said he, in relating the incident afterwards, "I thought I had power. I had the largest congregation in Chicago, and there were many conversions. I was in a sense satisfied. But right along those two godly women kept praying for me, and their earnest talk about anointing for special service set me thinking. I asked them to come and talk with me, and they poured out their hearts in prayer that I might receive the filling of the Holy Spirit. There came a great hunger into my soul. I did not know what it was. I began to cry out as I never did before. I really felt that I did not want to live if I could not have this power for service."

In October of 1871, the Great Chicago Fire destroyed Moody's church, home, and the dwellings of most of his members. His family had to flee for their lives, and, as Mr. Moody said, he saved nothing but his reputation and his Bible. "While Mr. Moody was in this mental and spiritual condition," said his son, "Chicago was laid in ashes. The great fire swept out of existence both Farwell Hall and Illinois Street Church. On Sunday night after the meeting, as Mr. Moody went homeward, he saw the glare of flames, and knew it meant ruin to Chicago. About one o'clock Farwell Hall was burned; and soon his church went down. Everything was scattered."

Mr. Moody went East to New York City to collect funds for the sufferers from the Chicago fire, but his heart and soul were crying out for the power from on high. "My heart was not in the work of begging," says he. "I could not appeal. I was crying all the time that God would fill me with His Spirit.

Well, one day, in the city of New York—oh, what a day!—I cannot describe it, I seldom refer to it; it is almost too sacred an experience to name. Paul had an experience of which he never spoke for fourteen years. I can only say that God revealed himself to me, and I had such an experience of His love that I had to ask Him to stay His hand. I went to preaching again. The sermons were not different; I did not present any new truths; and yet hundreds were converted. I would not now be placed back where I was before that blessed experience if you should give me all the world; it would be as the small dust of the balance." His soul was set on fire in such a way that his work would soon become a worldwide one.

His church was rebuilt within three months at a nearby location as the Chicago Avenue Church. Thousands of Sunday school scholars contributed five cents each to place a brick in the new edifice. His lay follower William Eugene Blackstone was a prominent American Zionist.

In the years after the fire, Moody's wealthy Chicago supporter J. A. Farwell attempted to persuade him to make his permanent home in Chicago, offering to build Moody and his family a new house. But the now famous Moody, also sought by supporters in New York, Philadelphia, and elsewhere, chose the tranquil farm he had purchased next door to his birthplace in Northfield, MA. He felt he could better recover from his lengthy and exhausting preaching trips in a rural setting.

Northfield became an important location in evangelical Christian history in the late 19th century as Moody organized summer conferences which were led and attended by prominent Christian preachers and evangelists from around the world. It was also in Northfield that Moody founded three schools which later merged into today's Northfield Mount Hermon School.

Great Britain

Desiring to learn more of the Scriptures from English Bible students, he visited England again in 1872. He did not expect to hold any meetings during this visit, but he accepted an invitation to preach at the Sunday morning and evening service at Arundel Square Congregational Church in the North part of London. In the evening, the power of the Spirit seemed to fall upon the congregation, and the inquiry room was crowded with persons seeking salvation. Next day he went to Dublin, Ireland, but an urgent telegram called him back to continue his meetings at the North London Church. He continued there for ten days and four hundred persons were added to the church. He was invited to Dublin and Newcastle but decided not to go at that time, and he returned to the United States.

Next year, at the invitation of two English friends, he started for England, accompanied by Sankey. His English friends had promised funds for the visit, but the money did not come and Moody borrowed enough to enable him to go to England. On arriving there, he learned that both of his friends had died. No door seemed open for him. But before leaving the United States he had received a letter from the Secretary of the YMCA at York, England, inviting him to address the young men there if he ever came to England. He and Sankey went to York, and began a series of meetings there which lasted for five weeks. Interest gradually increased until the meeting places were crowded half an hour before the time of service, and many souls decided for Christ.

The evangelists went from York to Sunderland, where they had still greater meetings than in York. The largest halls in the city had to be secured for the services. Their next series of meetings was in Newcastle. Here the meetings were gigantic, special trains bringing people from surrounding cities and towns. Here the evangelists published their first hymn book entitled *Gospel Hymns, No. 1*, which was followed by Numbers 2, 3, 4, 5, and 6. The books soon became popular all over Britain and have been a means of blessing to multitudes throughout the world. They marked a new era in the history of the Christian church. The royalties on them were at first devoted to a number of benevolent purposes, but afterwards to the founding and carrying on of Moody's great Bible schools at Northfield.

Other great meetings were held in Liverpool and many other British cities, and finally in London. On several occasions Moody filled stadiums with seating from 2,000 to 4,000 to capacity. This turnout continued throughout 1874 and 1875, with crowds of even greater thousands at all of his meetings.

Moody aided in the work of cross-cultural evangelism by promoting "The Wordless Book," a teaching tool that had been invented by Charles Spurgeon in 1866. In 1875 he added the fourth color—gold—to the design of the three-color evangelistic device to "represent Heaven." This "book" has been and is still used to teach uncounted thousands of illiterate people—young and old—around the globe about the gospel message.[2]

When the evangelists left Britain in 1875, the whole country had been stirred religiously as it had not been stirred since the days of Wesley and Whitefield. About 14,000 children attended the children's meeting in Liverpool. Over 600 ministers attended the closing services in London. Moody said that he had such a consciousness of the presence of God in the London meetings that "the people seemed as grasshoppers." Professor Henry Drummond said that Moody spoke to exactly "an acre of people" every meeting during his campaign in the East End of London.

On their return to the United States, Moody and Sankey held great meetings from Boston to New York, throughout New England and as far as San Francisco, and other West coast towns from Vancouver to San Diego. Crowds of 12,000 to 20,000 were just as common as in England. President Grant and some of his cabinet attended a meeting on January 19, 1876.

In 1881, they again visited Great Britain and conducted another gigantic evangelistic campaign. After these campaigns, Moody made repeated trips to Britain, and once he visited the Holy Land. He devoted much time to building up his great Bible schools at Northfield and in Chicago. During the World's Fair in Chicago, in 1893, he conducted great meetings in the largest halls in the city and in Forepaugh's Circus tent, with the assistance of famous preachers from all over the world. Millions heard the gospel preached during this campaign.

From the North of England the evangelists went to Scotland, and began a series of meetings in Edinburgh. Here they had one of the greatest series of meetings ever known in the world's history. No building was large enough to accommodate the immense throngs which flocked to their meetings. "Never, probably," says Professor Blaikie, "was Scotland so stirred; never was there so much expectation." During his visit to Scotland he was helped and encouraged by Andrew A. Bonar. The famous London Baptist preacher, Charles Spurgeon, invited him to speak and promoted him as well.

In 1883, Moody and Sankey visited Edinburgh and raised £10,000 for the building of a new home for the Carrubbers Close Mission. Moody later preached at the laying of the foundation stone for one of the few buildings on the Royal Mile which continues to be used for its original purpose and is now called the Carrubbers Christian Centre.

In Glasgow, Scotland, the evangelists had similar meetings to those at Edinburgh. At the closing service at the Crystal Palace, in the Botanic Gardens, the building was packed so tightly with people Moody could not enter, and there were still 20 to 30 thousand persons on the outside. Moody spoke to the great throng from the seat of a cab, and the choir led the singing from the roof of a nearby shed. When the Crystal Palace was filled with inquirers seeking salvation, there were still about 2,000 inquirers on the outside of the building. Moody probably addressed as many as 30,000 persons at one time in Edinburgh and as many as 40,000 in Glasgow.

D. L. Moody was undoubtedly one of the greatest evangelists of all time. The meetings held by Moody and Sankey were among the greatest the world has ever known. They were the means, under God, of arousing the church to new life and activity, and the means of sweeping tens of thousands of persons into the kingdom of God.

Moody's Influence in China and Sweden

Moody greatly influenced the cause of cross-cultural Christian missions after he met Hudson Taylor, the pioneer missionary to China. He actively supported the China Inland Mission and encouraged many of his congregation to volunteer for service overseas.

His influence was felt among Swedes despite the fact that he was of English heritage, had never visited Sweden or any Scandinavian country, and never spoke a word of the Swedish language. Nevertheless, he became a hero evangelist among Swedish Mission Friends in Sweden and the United States. News of Moody's large meeting campaigns in Great Britain from 1873–1875 traveled quickly to Sweden, making "Mr. Moody" a household name in homes of many Mission Friends. Moody's sermons published in Sweden were distributed in books, newspapers, and colporteur tracts, and led to the spread of Sweden's "Moody fever" from 1875–1880.

Moody's Death

Moody continued his evangelistic campaigns until his death in 1899. He preached his last sermon on November 16, 1899 in a gigantic hall in Kansas City, KS. While there, he was seized with heart trouble and returned home by train to Northfield. During the preceding several months, friends had observed he had added some thirty pounds to his already ample frame. Although his illness was never diagnosed, it has been speculated that he suffered congestive heart failure.
Among his last words were, "This is my triumph; this is my coronation day! I have been looking forward to it for years." This old world had lost its charm for him and for a long time he had been "homesick for Heaven."

His Last Moments and His Will

Another told how just before the last he said, "Can't a man die sitting up as well as lying down," and when the doctor said yes, they took him up and let him rest for a few moments in his chair, but it was only for a little while, and then they put him back again in his bed. It was the last time he was to rise, and he who told it said with a sob, "I cannot bring myself to realize that he has gone from us." Another told how, when he was aroused from his stupor and saw all his loved ones around him, he said in his old way, so characteristic of himself, "What's going on here," and when they told him that he had been worse for a little time, and that they had come to be with him, he closed his eyes and seemed to fall asleep again.

Still another told of the will he made, unlike any other will that any man had ever made. He gave the care of Mt. Hermon to his son, William R. Moody; the Northfield Young Ladies' School to the care of Paul, his son, a junior in Yale; the special oversight of the Bible Institute to Mrs. Fitt and her husband, Mr. A. P. Fitt, the latter having for years been Mr.

Moody's closest and most confidential helper, particularly in the Bible Institute in Chicago and the Colportage Library work. The Northfield Training School was to be the care of Mr. Ambert G. Moody, his nephew. And when something was said about Mrs. Moody, he had said she was the mother of them all, and they must all care for her. An old friend gave the account of his words to his boys when he said, "I have always been an ambitious man, not ambitious to lay up money, but ambitious to leave you all work to be done, which is the greatest heritage one can leave to his children."[1]

A Triumphant Passing Away:
More on Moody's Death

Still another gave the picture of his last hours. No more memorable sentences on one's deathbed have ever been spoken. It was just such a triumphant passing away as his dear friends would have wished. Where have you ever read better sayings than these?

"Is this dying? Why this is bliss. There is no valley. I have been within the gates. Earth is receding; Heaven is opening; God is calling; I must go."

And when he went away from them for a little time and came back, he said that he had seen his loved ones in Heaven, giving their names, and when it was suggested that he had been dreaming, he assured them it was not so, but that he had actually been within the gates of Heaven.

He died on December 22, surrounded by family. Already installed by Moody as leader of his Chicago Bible Institute, R. A. Torrey succeeded Moody as its president. Ten years after Moody's death, the Chicago Avenue Church was renamed The Moody Church in his honor, and the Chicago Bible Institute was likewise renamed Moody Bible Institute.

In this manner, his noble life went out, and though he is dead he continues to speak, and tens of thousands rise up to call him blessed. Such intimate associates as Mr. Ira D. Sankey, Mr. George C. Stebbins, Rev. George C. Needinam, Prof. W. W. White, Mr. William Phillips Hall, Mr. John R. Mott, Mr. Richard C. Morse, Rev. George A. Hall, and many others talked until the evening was gone, and then retired each to feel that his was a personal bereavement, because D. L. Moody was dead.

Moody's earthly remains were laid to rest on "Round Top," at his beloved Northfield. By his special request there were no emblems of mourning at his funeral services. It is estimated that no less than a hundred million people heard the gospel from his lips, and his schools are training many others to carry the glad tidings throughout the world.[2]

Words from those who were at Moody's Funeral

REV. A. T. PIERSON'S ADDRESS

"I want to say a word of Mr. Moody's entrance into Heaven. When he entered into Heaven there must have been an unusual commotion. I want to ask you today whether you can think of any other man of the last half-century whose coming so many souls would have welcomed at the gates of Heaven. It was a triumphal entrance into glory.

"No man 'who has been associated with him in Christian work has not seen that there is but one way to live, and that way to live wholly for God. The thing that D. L. Moody stood and will stand for centuries to come was his living only for God. He made mistakes, no doubt, and if any of us is without sin in this respect, we might cast a stone at him, but I am satisfied that the mistakes of D. L. Moody were the mistakes of a stream that overflowed its banks. It is a great deal better to be full and overflowing than to be empty and have nothing to overflow.

"I feel myself called today by the presence of God to give eye that what is left shall be consecrated more wholly to him. Mr. Moody, John Wanamaker, James Spurgeon (brother of Charles), and myself were born in the same year. Only two of us are still alive. John Wanamaker, let us still live wholly for God."

DR. J. WILBUR CHAPMAN'S ADDRESS

"I cannot bring myself to feel this afternoon that this service is a reality. It seems to me that we must awake from some dream and see again the face of this dear man of God, which we have so many times seen. It is a new picture to me this afternoon. I never before saw Mr. Moody with his eyes closed. They were always open, and it seemed to me open not only to see where he could help others, but where he could help me. His hands were always outstretched to help others. I never came near him without his helping me."

At this point the sun came through a crack in a blind, and the rays fell directly on Mr. Moody's face, and nowhere else in the darkened church did a single beam of sunshine fall.

"The only thing that seems natural is the sunlight now on his face. There was always a halo around him. I can only give a slight tribute of the help he has done me, I can only especially dedicate myself to God, that I, with others, may preach the Gospel he taught.

"When I was a student, Mr. Moody found me. I had no object in Christ. He pointed me to the hope in God; he saw my heart, and I saw his Saviour. I have had a definite life since then. When perplexities have arisen, from those lips came the words, 'Who are you doubting? If you believe in God's Word, who are you doubting?' I was a pastor, a preacher, without much result. One day Mr. Moody came to me, and, with one hand on my shoulder and the other on the open Word of God, he said: 'Young man, you had better get more of this into your life,' and when I became an evangelist myself, in perplexity I would still sit at his feet, and every perplexity would vanish just as mist before the rising sun. And, indeed, I never came without the desire to be a better man, and be more like him, as he was like Jesus Christ. If my own father were lying in the coffin I could not feel more the sense of loss."

More on Moody's Life plus His Conversion [3]

"I had never lost sight of Jesus Christ since the first night I met Him in the store in Boston. But for years I was only a nominal Christian, really believing that I could not work for God. No one had ever asked me to do anything."

This seems strange, in the light of the Great Commission of Mark 16:15. — Ray Comfort

---

"I went to Chicago, I hired five pews in a church, and used to go out on the street and pick up young men and fill these pews. I never spoke to those young men about their souls; that was the work of the elders, I thought. After working for some time like that, I started a mission Sabbath school. I thought numbers were everything, and so I worked for numbers. When the attendance ran below one thousand, it troubled me; and when it ran to twelve or fifteen hundred, I was elated. Still none were converted; there was no harvest. Then God opened my eyes.

"There was a class of young ladies in the school, who were, without exception, the most frivolous set of girls I ever met. One Sunday the teacher was ill, and I took that class. They laughed in my face, and I felt like opening the door and telling them all to get out and never come back. That week the teacher of the class came into the place where I worked. He was pale, and looked very ill. 'What is the trouble?' I asked. ' I have had another hemorrhage of my lungs. The doctor says I cannot live on Lake Michigan, so I am going to New York State. I suppose I am going home to die.'

"He seemed greatly troubled, and when I asked him the reason, he replied: 'Well, I have never led any of my class to Christ. I really believe I have done the girls more harm than good.' I had never heard any one talk like that before, and it set me thinking. After a while I said: 'Suppose you go and tell them how you feel. I will go with you in a carriage, if you want to go.'

"He consented, and we started out together. It was one of the best journeys I ever had on earth. We went to the house of one of the girls, called for her, and the teacher talked to her about her soul. There was no laughing then! Tears stood in her eyes before long. After he had explained the way of life, he suggested that we have prayer. He asked me to pray. True, I had never done such a thing in my life as to pray God to convert a young lady there and then. But we prayed, and God answered our prayer. We went to other houses. He would go upstairs, and be all out of breath, and he would tell the girls what he had come for. It wasn't long before they broke down, and sought salvation. When his strength gave out, I took him back to his lodgings. The next day we went out again. At the end of ten days he came to the store with his face literally shining.

"'Mr. Moody,' he said, the last one of my class has yielded herself to Christ.' I tell you we had a time of rejoicing. He had to leave the next night, so I called his class together that night for a prayer meeting, and there God kindled a fire in my soul that has never gone out. The height of my ambition had been to be a successful merchant, and, if I had known that meeting was going to take that ambition out of me, I might not have gone. But how many times I have thanked God since for that meeting! The dying teacher sat in the midst of his class, and talked with them, and read the fourteenth chapter of John. We tried to sing 'Blest Be the Tie That Binds,' after which we knelt down to prayer. I was just rising from my knees, when one of the class began to pray for her dying teacher. Another prayed, and another, and before we rose, the whole class had prayed. As I went out I said to myself: 'O, God, let me die rather than lose the blessing I have received to-night!'

"The next morning I went to the depot to say good-bye to that teacher. Just before the train started, one of the class came, and before long, without any pre-arrangement, they were all there. What a meeting that was! We tried to sing, but we broke down. The last we saw of that dying teacher, he was standing on the platform of the car, his finger pointing upward, telling that class to meet him in Heaven."

Don't be fooled into thinking that this teacher gave these girls the "God has a wonderful plan for your life" or there's a "God-shaped hole in your heart" message. This was a man who was dying. Such an experience tends to sober us and make us think of the next life, rather than this one. Back in those days it was normal to speak to people about their sins by opening up the Ten Commandments and preaching the Cross. We must get into the mindset of that teacher. We are all dying men and women and we need to speak to sinners about their sin and eternity, rather than of how they can find fulfillment in this life. – Ray Comfort

---

"I didn't know what this was going to cost me. I was disqualified for business; it had become distasteful to me. I had got a taste of another world, and cared no more for making money. For some days after, the greatest struggle of my life took place. Should I give up business and give myself to Christian work, or should I not? I have never regretted my choice. O, the luxury of leading someone out of the darkness of this world into the glorious light and liberty of the Gospel."[4]

In a Moody Biography: "Moody did not have television, the Internet, radios, cable TV, fax machines, mp3 players, email, nor did he put out a national magazine. He did most of his preaching on foot and preached in the open air."

In P.B. Bliss' Biography: "Moody's modus operandi was to preach in the open air from the steps of the nearby courthouse for about thirty minutes and then to urge the crowd into his meeting. Bliss and his wife, having heard of Moody but never having heard him, out for a stroll before Sunday evening services, happened onto the outdoor preaching."[5]

The six o'clock meeting at "Roundtop, known as the open air meeting, was largely attended, and to me exceedingly enjoyable. Mr. Moody sat beside me on the grass, and led in prayer just before the address. Elijah on Mount Carmel, pleading with his God was not nearer the heart of his Father in faith and acceptableness, I am sure, than he, as he led us all in prayer that beautiful evening. 'We had a fine meeting that night in the auditorium and several interesting addresses were made, after which, at Mr. Moody's kind invitation, we went to his house, where, in company with a number of others a social hour was much enjoyed.

Mr. Moody was not easily discouraged, nor unduly elated. With all the activity of his great soul, there was still a calmness and courage characteristic of him that at once inspired hope, and kept us all at our best all the days and nights of toil. It was my privilege to be associated with him in the Central Palace Hall, in New York City, where thousands of people assembled every day to listen to his preaching. It was an unusual meeting in many respects, beginning in the early morning and continuing without intermission, throughout the day, until ten o'clock at night. There were many interesting conversions in those meetings, and the words which went abroad throughout the land must have accomplished great things. At the hotel, many of his co-workers were entertained, and the brief intervals of personal conversation were always heartily enjoyed. He would invite us to his room in the morning where, with Mrs. Moody and his daughter and others, he engaged in a daily worship before beginning the duties of the day. Handing me one of Henry Drummond's books one day with an inscription in his own hand to Mrs. Wharton, he turned the leaves rapidly and said, "Look at this," and showed me a paragraph where Drummond speaks of passing to the end of a journey of life, and then, "Isn't that good, Wharton—going to the Father, going to the Father." He has gone to the Father; he went before we wanted him to go, and as it seems to us the burning and shining light was consumed all too soon. Still the Father called, and when he went away, he said we must not call him back, and we will not. He cannot return to us, but we may go to him, and in that blessed land we shall meet to part no more. Thanks be unto God, who giveth us the victory through our Lord Jesus Christ.[6]

Endnotes

1 From *The Life & Work of Dwight Lyman Moody* by the Rev. Wilbur Chapman, D.D.
2 Copied by Stephen Ross for WholesomeWords.org from *Deeper Experiences of Famous Christians* by J. Gilchrist Lawson. Anderson, Ind.: Warner Press, 1911.
3 Taken from: http://www.chinstitute.org/DAILYF/2003/04/daily-04-21-2003.shtml. More Details on Moody's Conversion taken from: Harvey, Moody 28-30 Moody's own narrative taken from: *The Life & Work of Dwight Lyman Moody* by the Rev. Wilbur Chapman, D.D.
4 From http://www.tjlbc.com/StreetQuotes.htm
5 http://www.wholesomewords.org/biography/biomoody4.html
6 From http://www.biblebelievers.com/moody/33.html

Illustration Portfolio

DWIGHT LYMAN MOODY
1837–1899

BIRTHPLACE OF D.L. MOODY AT NORTHFIELD, MASS.

D.L. MOODY'S MOTHER. FROM A PORTRAIT TAKEN IN 1867.

Illustration Portfolio

DWIGHT L. MOODY AT THE TIME OF LEAVING HOME FOR BOSTON.

D.L. Moody during early years in Chicago.

Mr. Moody at age 27: Sunday-school Worker.

Illustration Portfolio

Mr. and Mrs. D.L. Moody in 1864 and in 1869.

Home of D.L. Moody at Northfield.

Illustration Portfolio

ILLINOIS STREET CHURCH, CHICAGO.
FIRST BUILDING ERECTED BY MR. MOODY.
SCENE OF HIS EFFORTS BEFORE THE CHICAGO FIRE.

MOODY'S TABERNACLE
FIRST BUILDING ERECTED AFTER THE CHICAGO FIRE. OCCUPIED FOR TWO YEARS.

IRA D. SANKEY.

Illustration Portfolio

Exterior of Old Pennsylvania Railroad Depot, Philadelphia.

Interior of Old Pennsylvania Railroad Depot, Philadelphia.
Scene of the great meetings in Philadelphia.

The "Hippodrome," New York

Interior View of the "Hippodrome."
During the New York Mission.

Ira S. Sankey (center) on the Porch of Betsy Moody Cottage at Northfield.

Illustration Portfolio

Delegates of the Y.M.C.A. assembled in convention at Northfield.

MOODY GOLD

The Northfield Seminary Buildings, on the Connecticut River. Mr. Moody's Enduring Monument.

Illustration Portfolio

Interior of the Moody Auditorium at Northfield.

MOODY GOLD

Mr. Moody's study in his home at Northfield.

Illustration Portfolio

With Campers at Camp Northfield.

Mr. Moody hailing a friend.

Moody with Daughter and Grandaughter.

Illustration Portfolio

Mr. Moody as his townsfolk knew him.

Mr. and Mrs. Moody with Grandchildren.

MOODY GOLD

Absorbed in his correspondence.

Illustration Portfolio

Mr. Moody as he appeared in 1886.

Bible used by Mr. Moody for many years.

MOODY GOLD

The Old Judge Converted

I remember, as I was coming out of the daily prayer meeting in one of our American cities a few years ago, a lady said she wished to speak to me; her voice trembled with emotion, and I saw at once that she was heavily burdened by something or other. She said she had long been praying for her husband, and she wanted to know if I would go to see him; she thought it might do him some good. What is his name? "Judge _____," and she mentioned one of the most eminent politicians in the State.

"I have heard of him," I said; "I am afraid I need not go; he is a booked infidel; I cannot argue with him."

"That is not what he wants," said the lady. "He has had too much argument already. Go and speak to him about his soul."

I said I would, although I was not very hopeful. I went to his house, was admitted to his room, and introduced myself as having come to speak to him about salvation.

"Then you have come on a very foolish errand," said he; "there's no use in attacking me, I tell you that. I am proof against all these things, I don't believe in them."

Well, I saw it was no use arguing with him; so I said, "I'll pray for you, and I want you to promise me that when you are converted you'll let me know."

"Oh, yes, I'll let you know," he said in a tone of sarcasm. "Oh, yes, I'll let you know when I'm converted!" I left him, but I continued to pray for him.

Some time subsequently I heard that the old judge was converted. I was again preaching in that city a while after that, and when I had done talking the judge himself came to me, and said: "I promised I'd let you know when I was converted; I have come to tell you of it. Have you not heard of it?"

"Yes; but I would like to hear from you how it happened."

"Well," said the judge, "one night, some time after you called on me, my wife had gone to the meeting; there was no one in the house but the servants. I sat by the drawingroom fire, and I began to think: Suppose my wife is right, that there is a heaven and a hell; and suppose she is on the right way to heaven, where am I going? I just dismissed the thought. But a second thought came: Surely He who created me is able to teach me. Yes, I thought, that is so. Then why not ask Him? I struggled against it, but at last, though I was too proud to get down on my knees, I just said, 'Father, all is dark; Thou who created me canst teach me.'

"Somehow, the more I prayed the worse I felt. I was very sad. I did not wish my wife to come home and find me thus, so I slipped away to bed, and when she came into the room I pretended to be asleep. She got down on her knees and prayed. I knew she was praying for me, and that for many long years she had been doing so. I felt as if I could have jumped up and knelt beside her; but no, my proud heart would not let me, so I lay still, pretending to be asleep. But I didn't sleep that night. I soon changed my prayer; it was now, 'O God, save me; take away this terrible burden.'

"I didn't believe in Christ even yet. I thought I'd go right straight to the Father Himself. But the more I prayed I only became the more miserable; my burden grew heavier. The next morning I did not wish to see my wife, so I said 'I am not well, and wouldn't wait for breakfast.' I went to the office, and when the boy came I sent him home for a holiday. When the clerks came I told them they might go for the day. I closed the office doors: I wanted to be alone with God. I was almost frantic in my agony of heart. I cried to God to take away this load of sin. At last I fell on my knees, and cried, 'For Jesus Christ's sake take away this load of sin.' At length I went to my wife's pastor, who had been praying with her for my conversion for years, and the same minister who had prayed with my mother before she died. As I walked down the street the verse that my mother had taught me came into my mind, 'Whatsoever things ye desire, when ye pray, believe that ye receive them, and ye shall have them.'

"Well, I thought, I have asked God, and here I am going to ask a man. I won't go. I believe I am a Christian. I turned and went home. I met my wife in the hall as I entered. I caught her hand, and said, 'I am a Christian now.' She turned quite pale; she had been praying for twenty-one years for me, and yet she could not believe the answer had come. We went into our room, and knelt down by the very bedside where she had so often knelt to pray for her husband. There we erected our family altar; and for the first time our voices mingled in prayer. And I can only say that the last three months have been the happiest months ever I spent in my life."

Since then that judge has lived a consistent Christian life; and all because he came to God, asking for guidance.

From *Christ All in All*: D.L. Moody

The Qualifications for Soul Winning

Away in the United States, a young lady was sent to a boarding school, and was there led to Christ; not only so, but taught that she ought to work for Him. By-and-by she goes home, and now she seeks, in one way and another, to work for Him, but without finding how. She asks for a class in her church Sunday school, but the superintendent is obliged to tell her that he has already more than enough teachers.

One day, going along the street, she sees a little boy struck by his companion, and crying bitterly. She goes up and speaks to him; asks him what the trouble is? The boy thinks she is mocking him, and replies sullenly. She speaks kindly, tries to persuade him to go to Sunday school. He does not want to learn. She coaxes him to come and hear her and the rest singing there; and so the next Sunday he comes with her. She gets a corner seat in the school of well dressed scholars for herself and her charge. He sits and listens, full of wonder. On going home, he tells his mother he has been among the angels. At first at a loss, she becomes angry, when a question or two brings out that he has been to a Protestant Sunday school; and the father, on coming home, forbids his going back, on pain of flogging. Next Sunday, however, he goes, and is flogged, and so again, and yet again, till one Sunday, he begs to be flogged before going, that he may not be kept thinking of it all the time. The father relents a little, and promises him a holiday every Saturday afternoon, if he will not go to Sunday school. The lad agrees, sees his teacher, who offers to teach him then. How many wealthy young folks would give up their Saturdays to train one poor ragged urchin in the way of salvation? Some time after, at his work, the lad is on one of the railway cars. The train starts suddenly; he slips through, and the wheels pass over his legs; he asks the doctor if he will live to get home; it is impossible. "Then," says he, "tell father and mother that I am going to Heaven, and want to meet them there." Will the work she did seem little now to the young lady? Or is it nothing that even one thus grateful waits her yonder?

Sermon delivered by Dwight L. Moody in Dr. Bonar's church, Edinburgh, Scotland, 7th December, 1873.

The Ten Commandments

An Infidel's Testimony

It is related of a clever infidel that he sought an acquaintance with the truths of the Bible, and began to read at the books of Moses. He had been in the habit of sneering at the Bible, and in order to be able to refute arguments brought by Christian men, he made up his mind, as he knew nothing about it, to read the Bible and get some idea of its contents. After he had reached the Ten Commandments, he said to a friend:

"I will tell you what I used to think. I supposed that Moses was the leader of a horde of bandits; that, having a strong mind, he acquired great influence over a superstitious people; and that on Mount Sinai he played off some sort of fireworks to the amazement of his ignorant followers, who imagined in their fear and superstition that the exhibition was supernatural. I have been looking into the nature of that Law. I have been trying to see whether I could add anything to it, or take anything from it, so as to make it better. Sir, I cannot! It is perfect!

"The first Commandment directs us to make the Creator the object of our supreme love and reverence. That is right. If He be our Creator, Preserver, and supreme Benefactor, we ought to treat Him, and none other, as such. The second forbids idolatry. That certainly is right. The third forbids profanity. The fourth fixes a time for religious worship. If there be a God, He ought surely to be worshipped. It is suitable that there should be an outward homage significant of our inward regard. If God be worshipped, it is proper that some time should be set apart for that purpose, when all may worship Him harmoniously, and without interruption. One day in seven is certainly not too much, and I do not know that it is too little.

"The fifth Commandment defines the peculiar duties arising from family relations. Injuries to our neighbor are then classified by the moral Law. They are divided into offenses against life, chastity, property, and character; and I notice that the greatest offense in each class is expressly forbidden. Thus the greatest injury to life is murder; to chastity, adultery; to property, theft; to character, perjury. Now the greatest offense must include the least of the same kind. Murder must include the least of the same kind. Murder must include every injury to life; adultery every injury to purity, and so of the rest. And the moral code is closed and perfected by a command forbidding every improper desire in regard to our neighbors.

"I have been thinking. Where did Moses get that Law? I have read history. The Egyptians and the adjacent nations were idolaters; so were the Greeks and Romans; and the wisest or best Greeks or Romans never gave a code of morals like this. Where did Moses obtain that Law, which surpasses the wisdom and philosophy of the most enlightened ages? He lived at a period comparatively barbarous; but he has given a Law in which the learning and sagacity of all subsequent time can detect no flaw. Where did he obtain it? He could not have soared so far above his age as to have devised it himself. I am satisfied where he obtained it. It came down from heaven. It has convinced me of the truth of the religion of the Bible."

The former infidel remained to his death a firm believer in the truth of Christianity.

The Ten Commandments Continued

But though there is far too much of this frivolous, familiar use of God's name, the Commandment is broken a great deal more by profanity. Taking the name of God in vain is blasphemy. Is there a swearing man who reads this? What would you do if you were put into the balances of the sanctuary, if you had to step in opposite to this Third Commandment? Think a moment, have you been taking God's name in vain today?

I do not believe men would ever have been guilty of swearing unless God had forbidden it. They do not swear by their friends, their fathers or mothers, their wives or children. They want to show how they despise God's Law.

A great many men think there is nothing in swearing. Bear in mind that God sees something wrong in it, and He says He will not hold men guiltless, even though society does.

I met a man sometime ago who told me he had never sinned in his life. He was the first perfect man I had ever met. I thought I would question him, and began to measure him by the Law. I asked him: "Do you ever get angry?"

"Well," he said, "sometimes I do; but I have a right to do so. It is righteous indignation."

"Do you swear when you get angry?"

He admitted he did sometimes.

"Then," I asked, "are you ready to meet God?"

"Yes," he replied, "because I never mean anything when I swear."

Suppose I steal a man's watch and he comes after me.

"Yes," I say, "I stole your watch and pawned it, but I did not mean anything by it. I pawned it and spent the money, but I did nor mean anything by it."

You would smile at and deride such a statement.

Ah, friends! You cannot trifle with God in that way. Even if you swear without meaning it, it is forbidden by God. Christ said: "Every idle word that men shall speak, they shall give an account thereof in the day of judgment; for by thy words thou shalt be justified, and by thy words thou shalt be condemned" (Matthew 12:36, 37). You will be held accountable whether your words are idle or blasphemous.

More Insight from The Ten Commandments

When I was out west about thirty years ago, I was preaching one day in the open air, when a man drove up in a fine carriage, and after listening a little while to what I was saying, he put the whip to his fine looking steed, and away he went, I never expected to see him again, but the next night he came back, and he kept on coming regularly night after night.

I noticed that his forehead itched—you have noticed people who keep putting their hands to their foreheads?—he didn't want any one to see him shedding tears—of course not! It is not a manly thing to shed tears in a religious meeting, of course!

After the meeting I said to a gentleman: "Who is that man who drives up here every night? Is he interested?"

"Interested! I should think not! You should have heard the way he talked about you today."

"Well," I said, "that is a sign he is interested."

If no man ever has anything to say against you, your Christianity isn't worth much. Men said of the Master, "He has a devil," and Jesus said that if they had called the master of the house Beelzebub, how much more them of his household.

I asked where this man lived, but my friend told me not to go to see him, for he would only curse me. I said: "It takes God to curse a man; man can only bring curses on his own head." I found out where he lived and went to see him. He was the wealthiest man within a hundred miles of that place, and had a wife and seven beautiful children. Just as I got to his gate I saw him coming out of the front door. I stepped up to him and said: "This is Mr. _____, I believe?"

He said, "Yes, sir; that is my name." Then he straightened up and asked, "What do you want?"

"Well," I said, "I would like to ask you a question, if you won't be angry."

"Well, what is it?"

"I am told that God has blessed you above all men in this part of the country; that He has given you wealth, a beautiful Christian wife, and seven lovely children. I do not know if it is true, but I hear that all He gets in return is cursing and blasphemy"

He said, "Come in; come in." I went in.

"Now," he said, "what you said out there is true. If any man has a fine wife I am the man, and I have a lovely family of children, and God has been good to me. But do you know, we had company here the other night, and I cursed my wife at the table and did not know it till after the company had gone. I never felt so mean and contemptible in my life as when my wife told me of it. She said she wanted the floor to open and let her down out of her seat. If I have tried once, I have tried a hundred times to stop swearing. You preachers don't know anything about it."

"Yes," I said, "I know all about it; I have been a drummer."

"But," he said, "you don't know anything about a businessman's troubles. When he is harassed and tormented the whole time, he can't help swearing."

"Oh, yes," I said, "he can. I know something about it. I used to swear myself."

"What! You used to swear?" he asked; "how did you stop?"

"I never stopped."

"Why, you don't swear now, do you?"

"No; I have not sworn for years."

"How did you stop?"

"I never stopped. It stopped itself."

He said, "I don't understand this."

"No," I said, "I know you don't. But I came up to talk to you, so that you will never want to swear as long as you live."

I began to tell him about Christ in the heart; how that would take the temptation to swear out of a man.

"Well," he said, "how am I to get Christ?"

"Get right down here and tell Him what you want."

"But," he said, "I was never on my knees in my life. I have been cursing all the day, and I don't know how to pray or what to pray for."

"Well," I said, "it is mortifying to have to call on God for mercy when you have never used His name except in oaths; but He will not turn you away. Ask God to forgive you if you want to be forgiven."

Then the man got down and prayed—only a few sentences, but thank God, it is the short prayers, after all, which bring the quickest answers. After he prayed he got up and said: "What shall I do now?"

I said, "Go down to the church and tell the people there that you want to be an out-and-out Christian."

"I cannot do that," he said; "I never go to church except to some funeral."

"Then it is high time for you to go for something else," I said.

After a while he promised to go, but did not know what the people would say. At the next church prayer meeting, the man was there, and I sat right in front of him. He stood up and put his hands on the settee, and he trembled so much that I could feel the settee shake. He said:

"My friends, you know all about me. If God can save a wretch like me, I want to have you pray for my salvation."

That was thirty odd years ago. Sometime ago I was back in that town, and did not see him; but when I was in California, a man asked me to take dinner with him. I told him that I could not do so, for I had another engagement. Then he asked if I remembered him, and told me his name. "Oh," I said, "tell me, have you ever sworn since that night you knelt in your drawing room, and asked God to forgive you?"

"No," he replied, "I have never had a desire to swear since then. It was all taken away."

He was not only converted, but became an earnest, active Christian, and all these years has been serving God. That is what will take place when a man is born of the divine nature.

The Ten Commandments: A sermon delivered by D.L. Moody

May God give us more testimonies like this. Things like this delight me and bring me to tears. God bless D. L. Moody for his boldness, and may He make us just as bold. If you need help in this area, feel free to listen to free audios on www.livingwaters.com — Ray Comfort

Hell

I remember a few years ago, while the Spirit of God was working in my church, I closed the meeting one night by asking any that would like to become Christians to rise, and to my great joy, a man arose who had been anxious for some time. I went up to him and took him by the hand and shook it, and said, "I am glad to see you get up. You are coming out for the Lord now in earnest, are you not?"

"Yes," said he, "I think so. That is, there is only one thing in my way."

"What's that?" said I.

"Well," said he, "I lack moral courage. I confess to you that if such a man [naming a friend of his] had been here tonight I should not have risen. He would laugh at me if he knew of this, and I don't believe I have the courage to tell him."

"But," said I, "You have got to come out boldly for the Lord if you come out at all."

While I talked with him he was trembling from head to foot, and I believe the Spirit was striving earnestly with him. He came back the next night, and the next, and the next; the Spirit of God strove with him for weeks; it seemed as if he came to the very threshold of Heaven, and was almost stepping over into the blessed world. I never could find out any reason for his hesitation, except that he feared his old companions would laugh at him.

At last the Spirit of God seemed to leave him; conviction was gone. Six months from that time I got a message from him that he was sick and wanted to see me. I went to him in great haste. He was very sick, and thought he was dying. He asked me if there was any hope. Yes, I told him, God had sent Christ to save him; and I prayed with him.

Contrary to all expectations he recovered. One day I went down to see him. It was a bright, beautiful day, and he was sitting out in front of his house.

"You are coming out for God now, aren't you? You will be well enough soon to come back to our meetings again."

"Mr. Moody," said he, "I have made up my mind to become a Christian. My mind is fully made up to that, but I won't be one just now. I am going to Michigan to buy a farm and settle down, and then I will become a Christian."

"But you don't know yet that you will get well."

"O," said he, "I shall be perfectly well in a few days. I have got a new lease of life."

I pleaded with him, and tried every way to get him to take his stand. At last he said, "Mr. Moody, I can't be a Christian in Chicago. When I get away from Chicago, and get to Michigan, away from my friends and acquaintances who laugh at me, I will be ready to go to Christ."

"If God has not grace enough to save you in Chicago, he has not in Michigan" I answered.

At last he got a little irritated and said, "Mr. Moody, I'll take the risk," and so I left him.

I well remember the day of the week, Thursday, about noon, just one week from that very day, when I was sent for by his wife to come in great haste. I hurried there at once. His poor wife met me at the door, and I asked her what was the matter.

"My husband," she said, "has had a relapse; I have just had a council of physicians here, and they have all given him up to die."

"Does he want to see me?" I asked.

"No."

"Then why did you send for me?"

"I cannot bear to see him die in this terrible state of mind."

"What does he say?" I asked.

"He says his damnation is sealed, and he will be in hell in a little while."

I went in, and he at once fixed his eyes upon me. I called him by name, but he was silent. I went around to the foot of the bed, and looked in his face and said, "Won't you speak to me?", and at last he fixed that terrible deathly look upon me and said:

"Mr. Moody, you need not talk to me any more. It is too late. You can talk to my wife and children; pray for them; but my heart is as hard as the iron in that stove there. My damnation is sealed, and I shall be in hell in a little while."

I tried to tell him of Jesus' love and God's forgiveness, but he said, "Mr. Moody, I tell you there is no hope for me." And as I fell on my knees, he said, "You need not pray for me. My wife will soon be left a widow and my children will be fatherless; they need your prayers, but you need not pray for me."

I tried to pray, but it seemed as if my prayers didn't go higher than my head, and as if Heaven above me was like brass. The next day, his wife told me, he lingered until the sun went down, and from noon until he died all he was heard to say was, "The harvest is past, the summer is ended, and I am not saved." After lingering along for an hour he would say again those awful words, and just as he was expiring his wife noticed his lips quiver, and that he was trying to say something, and as she bent over him she heard him mutter, "The harvest is past, the summer is ended, and I am not saved." He lived a Christless life, he died a Christless death —we wrapped him in a Christless shroud, and bore him away to a Christless grave.

Are there some here that are almost persuaded to be Christians? Take my advice and don't let any thing keep you away. Fly to the arms of Jesus this hour. You can be saved if you will.

Hell: A sermon by D.L. Moody

Never be afraid to put the fear of God in those who prefer man's approval to God's. Open up the Commandments and speak plainly about the justice of death and hell. There is an insanity that blinds us to the reality of our personal demise. We think that death is something that happens to other people. Speak of its immanence for every one of us, and pray that God makes your words come alive. – Ray Comfort

Heaven – Its Hope

In England I was told of a lady who had been bedridden for years. She was one of those saints that God polishes up for the kingdom; for I believe that there are a good many saints in this world that we never hear about; we never see their names heralded through the press; they live very near the Master; they live very near Heaven; and I think it takes a great deal more grace to suffer God's will than it does to do God's will; and if a person lies on a bed of sickness, and suffers cheerfully, it is just as acceptable to God as if they went out and worked in his vineyard.

I am sure he means that they rejoice in their suffering. A Christian should give thanks for and in everything. See Romans 8:28. – Ray Comfort

Now, it was one of those saints, and a lady, who said that for a long time she used to have a great deal of pleasure in watching a bird that came to make its nest near her window. One year it came to make its nest, and it began to make it so low she was afraid something would happen to the young; and every day that she saw that bird busy at work making its nest, she kept saying, "O bird, build higher!" She could see that the bird was going to come to grief and disappointment. At last the bird got its nest done, and laid its eggs and hatched its young; and every morning the lady looked out to see if the nest was there, and she saw the old bird bringing food for the little ones, and she took a great deal of pleasure in looking at it. But one morning she woke up and she looked out and she saw nothing but feathers scattered all around, and she said, "Ah, the cat has got the old bird and all its young." It would have been a mercy to have torn that nest down. That is what God does for us very often just snatches things away before it is to late. Now, I think that is what we want to say to church people that if you build for time you will be disappointed. God says: Build up yonder. It is a good deal better to have life in Christ and God than any where else.

Heaven—Its Hope: A sermon by D.L. Moody

Lost and Found

While in Philadelphia a man with his wife came to our meetings. When he left the service, he wouldn't speak to his wife. She thought it was very strange but said nothing and went to bed thinking that in the morning he would be all right.

At breakfast, however, he would not speak a word. Well, she thought this strange, but she was sure he would have gotten over whatever was wrong with him by dinner.

The dinner hour arrived, and it passed without his saying a word.

At supper not a word escaped him, and he would not go with her to the meeting. Every day for a whole week the same thing went on.

But at the end of the week he could not stand it any longer, and he said to his wife, "Why did you write Mr. Moody and tell him all about me?"

"I never wrote to Mr. Moody in my life," said the wife.

"You did," he answered.

"You're mistaken. Why do you think that?"

"Well, then, I wronged you; but when I saw Mr. Moody picking me out among all those people and telling all about me, I was sure you must have written him."

It was the Son of Man seeking for him, my friends. And I hope there will be one here tonight who will feel that I am talking personally to him. May you feel that you are lost and that the Lord is seeking for you. When you feel this, it is an invitation for you to be saved.

I was in an infirmary not long since where a mother brought a little child in. She said, "Doctor, my little child's eyes have not been opened for several days, and I would like you to do something for them."

The doctor got some ointment and put it first on one, then on the other, and pulled them open. "Your child is blind," said the doctor. "He will never be able to see."

At first the mother couldn't take it in, but after a little she cast an appealing look upon that physician, and in a voice full of emotion, said, "Doctor, you don't mean to say that my child will never see again?"

"Your child has lost his sight, and he will never see again," replied the doctor.

That mother gave a scream and drew that child to her bosom. "O my darling child," sobbed the woman, "are you never to see the mother who gave you birth? never to see the world again?"

I could not keep back the tears when I saw the terrible agony of that woman when she realized the misfortune that had come upon her child.

A terrible calamity, to grope in total darkness through the world, never to look upon the bright sky, the green fields; never to see the faces of loved ones; but what was it in comparison to the loss of a soul? I would rather have my eyes plucked out of my head and go down to my grave in total blindness than lose my soul.

There is a very good story told of Rowland Hill and Lady Ann Erskine. You have seen it, perhaps, in print.

While he was preaching in a park in London to a large assemblage, she was passing in her carriage. She asked her footman when she saw Rowland Hill in the midst of the people: "Who is that man?"

"That is Rowland Hill, my lady."

She had heard a good deal about the man and thought she would like to see him, so she directed her coachman to drive near the platform. When the carriage came near, Rowland Hill saw the insignia of nobility and asked who that noble lady was. Upon being told, he said, "Stop, my friends, I have something to sell."

The idea of the preacher's becoming suddenly an auctioneer made the people wonder; but in the midst of a dead silence he said:

"I have more than a title to sell; I have more than the crown of Europe to sell—it is the soul of Lady Ann Erskine. Is there anyone here who bids for it? Yes, I hear a bid. Satan, Satan, what will you give?"

"I will give pleasure, honor, riches—yea, I will give the whole world for her soul."

"Do you hear another bid? Is there any other one? Do I hear another bid? Ah, I thought so; I hear another bid. The Lord Jesus Christ, what will You give for this soul?"

"I will give peace, joy, comfort that the world knows not of—yea, I will give eternal life."

"Lady Ann Erskine, you have heard the two bidders for your soul. Which will you accept?"

She ordered the door of her carriage to be opened. Then she came weeping from it and accepted the Lord Jesus Christ.

He, the great and mighty Savior, is a bidder for your soul tonight. He offers you riches and comfort, joy and peace here and eternal life hereafter, while Satan offers you what he cannot give.

Poor lost soul, which will you have? Christ will ransom your soul if you put your burden upon Him.

Lost and Found: A sermon by D.L. Moody

Repentance

My sister, I remember, told me her little boy said something naughty one morning, when his father said to him, "Sammy, go and ask your mother's forgiveness."

"I won't," replied the child.

"If you don't ask your mother's forgiveness I'll put you to bed." It was early in the morning, before he went to business, and the boy didn't think he would do it. He said "I won't" again. They undressed him and put him to bed.

The father came home at noon expecting to find his boy playing about the house. He didn't see him about, and asked his wife where he was. "In bed still." So he went up to the room, and sat down by the bed, and said: "Sammy, I want you to ask your mother's forgiveness." But the answer was "No."

The father coaxed and begged, but could not induce the child to ask forgiveness. The father went away, expecting certainly that when he came home that night the child would have got all over it. At night, however, when he got home he found the little fellow still in bed. He had lain there all day. He went to him and tried to get him to go to his mother, but it was no use. His mother went and was equally unsuccessful.

That father and mother could not sleep any that night. They expected every moment to hear the knock at their door by their little son. Now they wanted to forgive the boy. My sister told me it was just as if death had come into their home. She never passed through such a night. In the morning she went to him and said: "Now, Sammy, you are going to ask my forgiveness?" but the boy turned his face to the wall and wouldn't speak.

The father came home at noon and the boy was as stubborn as ever. It looked as though the child was going to conquer. It was for the good of the boy that they didn't want to give him his own way. It is a great deal better for us to submit to God than have our own way. Our own way will lead us to ruin; God's way leads to life everlasting. The father went off to his office, and that afternoon my sister went in to her son about four o'clock and began to reason with him, and, after talking for some time, she said, "Now, Sammy, say, 'Mother.'" "Mother," said the boy. "Now say 'for.'" "For." "Now just say 'give.'" And the boy repeated, "Give." "Me," said the mother. "Me," and the little fellow fairly leaped out of bed. "I have said it," he cried; "take me down to papa, so that I can say it to him."

Oh, sinner, go to Him and ask His forgiveness. This is repentance. It is coming in with a broken heart and asking the King of Heaven to forgive you. Don't say you can't. It is a lie. It is your stubborn will—it is your stubborn heart.

Repentance: A sermon by D.L. Moody

R. A. Torrey: Moody's Best Friend

Dr. R. A. Torrey was probably Moody's closest associate and friend. Dr. Torrey was the first superintendent of the Moody Bible Institute and set up a curriculum for that Bible Institute which has been a pattern for others like it. When Moody died, Torrey soon took worldwide lead in great citywide campaigns in Australia, England and the United States. In 1923, Dr. Torrey was asked to speak at a great memorial service on "Why God Used D. L. Moody," and this is that remarkable address about that amazing man, probably the greatest man of his generation, as Dr. Torrey said:

> Eighty-six years ago (February 5, 1837), there was born of poor parents in a humble farmhouse in Northfield, Massachusetts, a little baby who was to become the greatest man, as I believe, of his generation or of his century—Dwight L. Moody. After our great generals, great statesmen, great scientists and great men of letters have passed away and been forgotten, and their work and its helpful influence has come to an end, the work of D. L. Moody will go on, and its saving influence continue and increase, bringing blessing not only to every state in the Union but to every nation on Earth. Yes, it will continue throughout the ages of eternity.
>
> My subject is "Why God Used D. L. Moody," and I can think of no subject upon which I would rather speak. For I shall not seek to glorify Mr. Moody, but the God who by His grace, His entirely unmerited favor, used him so mightily, and the Christ who saved him by His atoning death and resurrection life, and the Holy Spirit who lived in him and wrought through him and who alone made him the mighty power that he was to this world.
>
> Furthermore, I hope to make it clear that the God who used D. L. Moody in his day is just as ready to use you and me, in this day, if we, on our part, do what D. L. Moody did, which was what made it possible for God to so abundantly use him. The whole secret of why D. L. Moody was such a mightily used man you will find in Psalm 62:11: "God hath spoken once; twice have I heard this; that POWER BELONGETH UNTO GOD." I am glad it does. If D. L. Moody had any power, and he had great power, he got it from God.
>
> The first thing that accounts for God's using D. L. Moody so mightily was that he was a fully surrendered man. Every ounce of that two hundred and eighty pound body of his belonged to God; everything he was and everything he had,

belonged wholly to God. Now, I am not saying that Mr. Moody was perfect; he was not. If I attempted to, I presume I could point out some defects in his character. It does not occur to me at this moment what they were; but I am confident that I could think of some, if I tried real hard.

The first month I was in Chicago, we were having a talk about something upon which we very widely differed, and Mr. Moody turned to me very frankly and very kindly and said in defense of his own position: "Torrey, if I believed that God wanted me to jump out of that window, I would jump." I believe he would. If he thought God wanted him to do anything, he would do it. He belonged wholly, unreservedly, unqualifiedly, entirely, to God.

Henry Varley, a very intimate friend of Mr. Moody in the earlier days of his work, loved to tell how he once said to him: "It remains to be seen what God will do with a man who gives himself up wholly to Him." I am told that when Mr. Henry Varley said that, Mr. Moody said to himself: "Well, I will be that man." And I, for my part, do not think "it remains to be seen" what God will do with a man who gives himself up wholly to Him. I think it has been seen already in D. L. Moody.

There are thousands and tens of thousands of men and women in Christian work, brilliant men and women, rarely gifted men and women, men and women who are making great sacrifices, men and women who have put all conscious sin out of their lives, yet who, nevertheless, have stopped short of absolute surrender to God, and therefore have stopped short of fullness of power. But Mr. Moody did not stop short of absolute surrender to God; he was a wholly surrendered man, and if you and I are to be used, you and I must be wholly surrendered men and women.

The second secret of the great power exhibited in Mr. Moody's life was that Mr. Moody was in the deepest and most meaningful sense a man of prayer. People oftentimes say to me: "Well, I went many miles to see and to hear D. L. Moody, and he certainly was a wonderful preacher." Yes, D. L. Moody certainly was a wonderful preacher; taking it all in all, the most wonderful preacher I have ever heard, and it was a great privilege to hear him preach as he alone could preach; but out of a very intimate acquaintance with him I wish to testify that he was a far greater pray-er than he was preacher. Time and time again, he was confronted by obstacles that seemed insurmountable, but he always knew the way to surmount and to overcome all difficulties. He knew the way to bring to pass anything that needed to be brought to pass. He knew and believed in the deepest depths of his soul that "nothing was too hard for the Lord" and that prayer could do anything that God could do.

Often times Mr. Moody would write me when he was about to undertake some new work, saying: "I am beginning work in such and such a place on such and such a day; I wish you would get the students together for a day of fasting and prayer." And often I have taken those letters and read them to the students in the lecture room and said: "Mr. Moody wants us to have a day of fasting and prayer, first for God's blessing on our own souls and work, and then for God's blessing on him and his work." Often we were gathered in the lecture room far into the night—sometimes till one, two, three, four or even five o'clock in the morning, crying to God, just because Mr. Moody urged us to wait upon God until we received His blessing. How many men and women I have known whose lives and characters have been transformed by those nights of prayer and who have wrought mighty things in many lands because of those nights of prayer!

One day Mr. Moody drove up to my house at Northfield and said: "Torrey, I want you to take a ride with me." I got into the carriage, and we drove out toward Lover's Lane, talking about some great and unexpected difficulties that had arisen in regard to the work in Northfield and Chicago, and in connection with other work that was very dear to him. As we drove along, some black storm clouds lay ahead of us, and then suddenly, as we were talking, it began to rain. He drove the horse into a shed near the entrance to Lover's Lane to shelter the horse, and then laid the reins upon the dashboard and said: "Torrey, pray;" and then, as best I could, I prayed, while he in his heart joined me in prayer. And when my voice was silent he began to pray. Oh, I wish you could have heard that prayer! I shall never forget it, so simple, so trustful, so definite and so direct and so mighty.

When the storm was over and we drove back to town, the obstacles had been surmounted, and the work of the schools, and other work that was threatened, went on as it had never gone on before, and it has gone on until this day. As we drove back, Mr. Moody said to me: "Torrey, we will let the other men do the talking and the criticizing, and we will stick to the work that God has given us to do, and let Him take care of the difficulties and answer the criticisms."

On one occasion Mr. Moody said to me in Chicago: "I have just found, to my surprise, that we are twenty thousand dollars behind in our finances for the work here and in Northfield, and we must have that twenty thousand dollars, and I am going to get it by prayer." He did not tell a soul who had the ability to give a penny of the twenty thousand dollars' deficit, but looked right to God and said: "I need twenty thousand dollars for my work; send me that money in such a way that I will know it comes straight from Thee." And God heard that prayer. The money came in such a way that it was clear that it came from God in direct answer to prayer.

The third secret of Mr. Moody's power, or the third reason why God used D. L. Moody, was because he was a deep and practical student of the Word of God. Nowadays it is often said of D. L. Moody that he was not a student. I wish to say that he was a student; most emphatically he was a student. He was not a student of psychology; he was not a student of anthropology—I am very sure he would not have known what that word meant; he was not a student of biology; he was not a student of philosophy; he was not even a student of theology, in the technical sense of the term; but he was a student, a profound and practical student of the one Book that is more worth studying than all other books in the world put together; he was a student of the Bible.

Every day of his life, I have reason for believing, he arose very early in the morning to study the Word of God, way down to the close of his life. Mr. Moody used to rise about four o'clock in the morning to study the Bible. He would say to me: "If I am going to get in any study, I have got to get up before the other folks get up;" and he would shut himself up in a remote room in his house, alone with his God and his Bible.

I shall never forget the first night I spent in his home. He had invited me to take the superintendency of the Bible Institute. and I had already begun my work; I was on my way to some city in the East to preside at the International Christian Workers' Convention. He wrote me saying: "Just as soon as the Convention is over, come up to Northfield." He learned when I was likely to arrive and drove over to South Vernon to meet me.

That night he had all the teachers from the Mount Hermon School and from the Northfield Seminary come together at the house to meet me, and to talk over the problems of the two schools. We talked together far on into the night, and then, after the principals and teachers of the schools had gone home, Mr. Moody and I talked together about the problems a while longer. It was very late when I got to bed that night, but very early the next morning, about five o'clock, I heard a gentle tap on my door. Then I heard Mr. Moody's voice whispering: "Torrey, are you up?" I happened to be; I do not always get up at that early hour but I happened to be up that particular morning. He said: "I want you to go somewhere with me," and I went down with him. Then I found out that he had already been up an hour or two in his room studying the Word of God.

It was largely because of his thorough knowledge of the Bible, and his practical knowledge of the Bible, that Mr. Moody drew such immense crowds. On "Chicago Day," in October, 1893, none of the theaters of Chicago dared to open because it was expected that everybody in Chicago would go on that day to the World's Fair; and, in point of fact, something like four hundred thousand people did pass through the gates of the Fair that day. Everybody in Chicago was expected to be at that end of the city on that day. But Mr. Moody said to me: "Torrey, engage the Central Music Hall and announce meetings from nine o'clock in the morning till six o'clock at night."

"Why," I replied, "Mr. Moody, nobody will be at this end of Chicago on that day; not even the theaters dare to open; everybody is going down to Jackson Park to the Fair; we cannot get anybody out on this day."

Mr. Moody replied: "You do as you are told;" and I did as I was told and engaged the Central Music Hall for continuous meetings from nine o'clock in the morning till six o'clock at night. But I did it with a heavy heart; I thought there would be poor audiences. I was on the program at noon that day. Being very busy in my office about the details of the campaign, I did not reach the Central Music Hall till almost noon. I thought I would have no trouble in getting in. But when I got almost to the Hall I found to my amazement that not only was it packed but the vestibule was packed and the steps were packed, and there was no getting anywhere near the door; and if I had not gone round and climbed in a back window they would have lost their speaker for that hour. But that would not have been of much importance, for the crowds had not gathered to hear me; it was the magic of Mr. Moody's name that had drawn them. And why did they long to hear Mr. Moody? Because they knew that while he was not versed in many of the philosophies and fads and fancies of the day, he did know the one Book that this old world most longs to know —the Bible.

During all the months of the World's Fair in Chicago, no one could draw such crowds as Mr. Moody. Judging by the papers, one would have thought that the great religious event in Chicago at that time was the World's Congress of Religions. One very gifted man of letters in the East was invited to speak at this Congress. He saw in this invitation the opportunity of his life and prepared his paper, the exact title of which I do not now recall, but it was something along the line of "New Light on the Old Doctrines." He prepared the paper with great care, and then sent it around to his most trusted and gifted friends for criticisms. These men sent it back to him with such recommendations as they had to suggest. Then he rewrote the paper, incorporating as many of the suggestions and criticisms as seemed wise. Then he sent it around for further criticisms. Then he wrote the paper a third time, and had it, as he trusted, perfect. He went on to Chicago to meet this coveted opportunity of speaking at the World's Congress of Religions.

It was at eleven o'clock on a Saturday morning (if I remember correctly) that he was to speak. He stood outside the door of the platform waiting for the great moment to arrive, and as the clock struck eleven he walked on to the platform to face a magnificent audience of eleven women and two men! But there was not a building anywhere in Chicago that would accommodate the very same day the crowds that would flock to hear Mr. Moody at any hour of the day or night.

The fourth reason why God continuously, through so many years, used D.L. Moody was because he was a humble man. I think D. L. Moody was the humblest man I ever knew in all my life. He loved to quote the words of another; "Faith gets the most; love works the most; but humility keeps the most."

He himself had the humility that keeps everything it gets. As I have already said, he was the most humble man I ever knew, i.e., the most humble man when we bear in mind the great things that he did, and the praise that was lavished upon him. Oh, how he loved to put himself in the background and put other men in the foreground. How often he would stand on a platform with some of us little fellows seated behind him and as he spoke he would say: "There are better men coming after me." As he said it, he would point back over his shoulder with his thumb to the "little fellows." I do not know how he could believe it, but he really did believe that the others that were coming after him were really better than he was. He made no pretense to a humility he did not possess. In his heart of hearts he constantly underestimated himself, and overestimated others. He really believed that God would use other men in a larger measure than he had been used.

Mr. Moody loved to keep himself in the background. At his conventions at Northfield, or anywhere else, he would push the other men to the front and, if he could, have them do all the preaching—McGregor, Campbell Morgan, Andrew Murray, and the rest of them. The only way we could get him to take any part in the program was to get up in the convention and move that we hear D. L. Moody at the next meeting. He continually put himself out of sight.

God used D. L. Moody, I think, beyond any man of his day; but it made no difference how much God used him, he never was puffed up.

One day, speaking to me of a great New York preacher, now dead, Mr. Moody said: "He once did a very foolish thing, the most foolish thing that I ever knew a man, ordinarily so wise as he was, to do. He came up to me at the close of a little talk I had given and said: 'Young man, you have made a great address tonight.'" Then Mr. Moody continued: "How foolish of him to have said that! It almost turned my head." But, thank God, it did not turn his head, and even when pretty much all the ministers in England, Scotland and Ireland, and many of the English bishops were ready to follow D. L. Moody wherever he led, even then it never turned his head one bit. He would get down on his face before God, knowing he was human, and ask God to empty him of all self-sufficiency. And God did.

The fifth secret of D. L. Moody's continual power and usefulness was his entire freedom from the love of money. Mr. Moody might have been a wealthy man, but money had no charms for him. He loved to gather money for God's work; he refused to accumulate money for himself. He told me during the World's Fair that if he had taken, for himself, the royalties on the hymnbooks which he had published, they would have amounted, at that time, to a million dollars. But Mr. Moody refused to touch the money. He had a perfect right to take it, for he was responsible for the publication of the books and it was his money that went into the publication of the first of them.

Mr. Sankey had some hymns that he had taken with him to England and he wished to have them published. He went to a publisher (I think Morgan & Scott) and they declined to publish them, because, as they said, Philip Phillips had recently been over and published a hymnbook, and it had not done well. However, Mr. Moody had a little money, and he said that he would put it into the publication of these hymns in cheap form; and he did. The hymns had a most remarkable and unexpected sale; they were then published in book form and large profits accrued. The financial results were offered to Mr. Moody, but he refused to touch them. "But," it was urged on him, "the money belongs to you;" but he would not touch it.

In a certain city to which Mr. Moody went in the latter years of his life, and where I went with him, it was publicly announced that Mr. Moody would accept no money whatever for his services. Now, in point of fact, Mr. Moody was dependent, in a measure, upon what was given him at various services; but when this announcement was made, Mr. Moody said nothing, and left that city without a penny's compensation for the hard work he did there; and, I think, he paid his own hotel bill. And yet a minister in that very city came out with an article in a paper, which I read, in which he told a fairy tale of the financial demands that Mr. Moody made upon them, which story I knew personally to be absolutely untrue. Millions of dollars passed into Mr. Moody hands, but they passed through; they did not stick to his fingers.

His Consuming Passion for the Salvation of the Lost

The sixth reason why God used D. L. Moody was because of his consuming passion for the salvation of the lost. Mr. Moody made the resolution, shortly after he himself was saved, that he would never let twenty-four hours pass over his head without speaking to at least one person about his soul. His was a very busy life, and sometimes he would forget his resolution until the last hour, and sometimes he would get out of bed, dress, go out and talk to someone about his soul in order that he might not let one day pass without having definitely told at least one of his fellow mortals about his need and the Savior who could meet it.

One night Mr. Moody was going home from his place of business. It was very late, and it suddenly occurred to him that he had not spoken to one single person that day about accepting Christ. He said to himself: "Here's a day lost. I have not spoken to anyone today, and I shall not see anybody at this late hour." But as he walked up the street he saw a man standing under a lamppost. The man was a perfect stranger to him, though it turned out afterwards the man knew who Mr. Moody was. He stepped up to this stranger and said: "Are you a Christian?"

The man replied: "That is none of your business, whether I am a Christian or not. If you were not a sort of a preacher I would knock you into the gutter for your impertinence."

Mr. Moody said a few earnest words and passed on. The next day that man called upon one of Mr. Moody's prominent business friends and said to him: "That man Moody of yours over on the North Side is doing more harm than he is good. He has got zeal without knowledge. He stepped up to me last night, a perfect stranger, and insulted me. He asked me if I were a Christian, and I told him it was none of his business and if he were not a sort of a preacher I would knock him into the gutter for his impertinence. He is doing more harm than he is good. He has got zeal without knowledge."

Mr. Moody's friend sent for him and said: "Moody, you are doing more harm than you are good; you've got zeal without knowledge: you insulted a friend of mine on the street last night. You went up to him, a perfect stranger, and asked him if he were a Christian, and he tells me if you had not been a sort of a preacher he would have knocked you into the gutter for your impertinence. You are doing more harm than you are good; you have got zeal without knowledge.

Mr. Moody went out of that man's office somewhat crestfallen. He wondered if he were not doing more harm than he was good, if he really had zeal without knowledge.

Weeks passed by. One night Mr. Moody was in bed when he heard a tremendous pounding at his front door. He jumped out of bed and rushed to the door. He thought the house was on fire. He thought the man would break down the door. He opened the door and there stood this man. He said: "Mr.

Moody, I have not had a good night's sleep since that night you spoke to me under the lamppost, and I have come around at this unearthly hour of the night for you to tell me what I have to do to be saved." Mr. Moody took him in and told him what to do to be saved. Then he accepted Christ, and when the Civil War broke out, he went to the front and laid down his life fighting for his country.

Another night, Mr. Moody got home and had gone to bed before it occurred to him that he had not spoken to a soul that day about accepting Christ. "Well," he said to himself, "it is no good getting up now; there will be nobody on the street at this hour of the night." But he got up, dressed and went to the front door. It was pouring rain. "Oh," he said, "there will be no one out in this pouring rain."

Just then he heard the patter of a man's feet as he came down the street, holding an umbrella over his head. Then Mr. Moody darted out and rushed up to the man and said: "May I share the shelter of your umbrella?" "Certainly," the man replied. Then Mr. Moody said: "Have you any shelter in the time of storm?" and preached Jesus to him. Oh, men and women, if we were as full of zeal for the salvation of souls as that, how long would it be before the whole country would be shaken by the power of a mighty, God-sent meeting?

One day in Chicago—the day after the elder Carter Harrison was shot, when his body was lying in state in the City Hall—Mr. Moody and I were riding up Randolph Street together in a streetcar right alongside of the City Hall. The car could scarcely get through because of the enormous crowds waiting to get in and view the body of Mayor Harrison. As the car tried to push its way through the crowd, Mr. Moody turned to me and said: "Torrey, what does this mean?"

"Why," I said, "Carter Harrison's body lies there in the City Hall, and these crowds are waiting to see it."

Then he said: "This will never do, to let these crowds get away from us without preaching to them; we must talk to them. You go and hire Hooley's Opera House (which was just opposite the City Hall) for the whole day." I did so. The meetings began at nine o'clock in the morning, and we had one continuous service from that hour until six in the evening, to reach those crowds.

Mr. Moody was a man on fire for God. Not only was he always "on the job" himself, but he was always getting others to work as well. He once invited me down to Northfield to spend a month there with the schools, speaking first to one school and then crossing the river to the other. I was obliged to use the ferry a great deal; it was before the present bridge was built at that point.

One day he said to me: "Torrey, did you know that that ferryman that ferries you across every day was unconverted?" He did not tell me to speak to him, but I knew what he meant. When some days later it was told him that the ferryman was saved, he was exceedingly happy.

Once, when walking down a certain street in Chicago, Mr. Moody stepped up to a man, a perfect stranger to him, and said: "Sir, are you a Christian?" "You mind your own business," was the reply. Mr. Moody replied: "This is my business." The man said, "Well, then, you must be Moody." Out in Chicago they used to call him in those early days "Crazy Moody," because day and night he was speaking to everybody he got a chance to speak to about being saved.

One time he was going to Milwaukee, and in the seat that he had chosen sat a traveling man. Mr. Moody sat down beside him and immediately began to talk with him. "Where are you going?" Mr. Moody asked. When told the name of the town he said: "We will soon be there; we'll have to get down to business at once. Are you saved?" The man said that he was not, and Mr. Moody took out his Bible and there on the train showed him the way of salvation. Then he said: "Now, you must take Christ." The man did; he was converted right there on the train.

Dwight L. Moody

Most of you have heard, I presume, the story President Wilson used to tell about D. L. Moody. Ex-President Wilson said that he once went into a barber shop and took a chair next to the one in which D. L. Moody was sitting, though he did not know that Mr. Moody was there. He had not been in the chair very long before, as ex-President Wilson phrased it, he "knew there was a personality in the other chair," and he began to listen to the conversation going on; he heard Mr. Moody tell the barber about the Way of Life, and President Wilson said, "I have never forgotten that scene to this day." When Mr. Moody was gone, he asked the barber who he was; when he was told that it was D. L. Moody, President Wilson said: "It made an impression upon me I have not yet forgotten."

On one occasion in Chicago Mr. Moody saw a little girl standing on the street with a pail in her hand. He went up to her and invited her to his Sunday school, telling her what a pleasant place it was. She promised to go the following Sunday, but she did not do so. Mr. Moody watched for her for weeks, and then one day he saw her on the street again, at some distance from him. He started toward her, but she saw him, too, and started to run away. Mr. Moody followed her. Down she went one street, Mr. Moody after her; up she went another street, Mr. Moody after her, through an alley, Mr. Moody still following; out on another street, Mr. Moody after her; then she dashed into a saloon and Mr. Moody dashed after her. She ran out the back door and up a flight of stairs, Mr. Moody still following; she dashed into a room, Mr. Moody following; she threw herself under the bed and Mr. Moody reached under the bed and pulled her out by the foot, and led her to Christ. He found that her mother was a widow who had once seen better circumstances, but had gone down until now she was living over this saloon. She had several children. Mr. Moody led the mother and all the family to Christ. Several of the children were prominent members of the Moody Church until they moved away, and afterwards became prominent in churches elsewhere. This particular child, whom he pulled from underneath the bed, was, when I was the pastor of the Moody Church, the wife of one of the most prominent officers in the church.

Only two or three years ago, as I came out of a ticket office in Memphis, Tennessee, a fine looking young man followed me. He said: "Are you not Dr. Torrey?" I said, "Yes." He said: "I am so and so." He was the son of this woman. He was then a traveling man, and an officer in the church where he lived. When Mr. Moody pulled that little child out from under the bed by the foot, he was pulling a whole family into the Kingdom of God, and eternity alone will reveal how many succeeding generations he was pulling into the Kingdom of God.

D.L. Moody's consuming passion for souls was not for the souls of those who would be helpful to him in building up his work here or elsewhere; his love for souls knew no class limitations. He was no respecter of persons; it might be an earl or a duke or it might be an ignorant colored boy on the street; it was all the same to him; there was a soul to save and he did what lay in his power to save that soul.

A friend once told me that the first time he ever heard of Mr. Moody was when Mr. Reynolds of Peoria told him that he once found Mr. Moody sitting in one of the squatters' shanties that used to be in that part of the city toward the lake, which was then called, "The Sands," with a black boy on his knee, a tallow candle in one hand and a Bible in the other, and Mr. Moody was spelling out the words (for at that time the boy could not read very well) of certain verses of Scripture, in an attempt to lead that ignorant black boy to Christ.

From http://www.whatsaiththescripture.com/Voice/Why.God.Used.D.L.Moody.html

D. L. Moody Quotes

"We are told to let our light shine, and if it does, we won't need to tell anybody it does. Lighthouses don't fire cannons to call attention to their shining—they just shine."

"There are many of us that are willing to do great things for the Lord, but few of us are willing to do little things

---

This is the key to having God open doors of opportunity. If you want to preach to large crowds, prove yourself at one-to-one. Wash the saints' feet. Be a servant. Love the lost. – Ray Comfort

---

"Either these [unsaved] people are to be evangelized, or the leaven of communism and infidelity will assume such enormous proportions that it will break you in a reign of terror such as this country has never known."

"Some day you will read in the papers that D.L. Moody of East Northfield, is dead. Don't you believe a word of it! At that moment I shall be more alive than I am now; I shall have gone up higher, that is all, out of this old clay tenement into a house that is immortal—a body that death cannot touch, that sin cannot taint; a body fashioned like unto His glorious body."

"I was born of the flesh in 1837. I was born of the Spirit in 1856. That which is born of the flesh may die. That which is born of the Spirit will live forever."

"Henry Varley, a very intimate friend of Mr. Moody in the earlier days of his work, loved to tell how he once said to him: *"It remains to be seen what God will do with a man who gives himself up wholly unto Him."* When Mr. Henry Varley said that Mr. Moody said to himself: *"Well I will be that man."*

"There's no better book with which to defend the Bible than the Bible itself."

"There are many of us that are willing to do great things for the Lord, but few of us are willing to do little things."

"A rule I have had for years is: to treat the Lord Jesus Christ as a personal friend. His is not a creed, a mere doctrine, but it is He himself we have."

"Where one man reads the Bible, a hundred read you and me."

"We talk about Heaven being so far away. It is within speaking distance to those who belong there. Heaven is a prepared place for a prepared people."

"I know the Bible is inspired because it inspires me"

"God never made a promise that was too good to be true."

"Death may be the King of terrors, but Jesus is the King of kings!"

"A man ought to live so that everybody knows he is a Christian—and most of all, his family ought to know."

"Character is what a man is in the dark."

Dwight L. Moody

It is also what we do in the darkness of the imagination. The essence of a godly character is the fear of the Lord.
— *Ray Comfort*

"God doesn't seek for golden vessels, and does not ask for silver ones, but He must have clean ones."

"The Bible will keep you from sin, or sin will keep you from the Bible."

"It is a masterpiece of the devil to make us believe that children cannot understand religion. Would Christ have made a child the standard of faith if He had known that it was not capable of understanding His words?"

"Either these [unsaved] people are to be evangelized, or the leaven of communism and infidelity will assume such enormous proportions that it will break you in a reign of terror such as this country has never known."

"Church attendance is as vital to a disciple as a transfusion of rich, healthy blood to a sick man."

"Preparation for old age should begin not later than one's teens. A life which is empty of purpose until sixty-five will not suddenly become filled on retirement."

"Where I was born and where and how I have lived is unimportant. It is what I have done with where I have been that should be of interest."

"Never think that Jesus commanded a trifle, nor dare to trifle with anything He has commanded."

"Give me a man who says this one thing I do, and not those fifty things I dabble in."

"No man can resolve himself into Heaven."

The Gospel Awakening

Is it well to number converts? Elijah got into trouble by trying to number Israel. It is best to let, the Lord keep the record. It makes me creep all over to hear a man tell how many he has converted. It is best not to triumph.

> *This is a wonderful quote. I am always amazed at how many evangelists and preachers seem to have access to the Book of Life. Such numbering reveals a lack of understanding to the nature of true and false conversion. Make sure you freely listen to "True and False Conversion" on www.livingwaters. com — Ray Comfort*

Is there any danger starting men into the work too young? There is a good deal of danger, in not starting them to work soon enough. Pitt was in Parliament at 21 and was Prime Minister at 32. Napoleon was young and Alexander had conquered the world at 32. There is danger sometimes in flattering young men who are at work for Christ. Spiritual pride is a very great injury. The young men in Chicago could be used to good advantage. They could go out and talk seven nights in the week while the minister preached but one. And these young men could reach men who could not be approached by anybody else.

Do you believe in open-air preaching? Yes; but not every man who can talk is fit to preach to open-air audiences. It needs a peculiar talent to go there. He wants to have tact, to know how to get along with these people. These meetings were attended by shrewd men, infidels and skeptics, and they were always ready to trip up the preacher. The man preaching to open-air audiences should not allow himself to be drawn into controversy.

The Qualifications for Soul-Winning

God had no children too weak, but a great many too strong to make use of. God stands in no need of our strength or wisdom, but of our ignorance, of our weakness; let us but give these to Him, and He can make use of us in winning souls.

Now we all want to shine; the mother wishes it for her boy, when she sends him to school, the father for his lad, when he goes off to college; and here God tells us who are to shine—not statesmen, or warriors, or such like, that shine but for a season, but such as will shine forever and ever;

those, namely, who win souls to Christ; the little boy even who persuades one to come to Christ.

Paul counts up five things (1 Corinthians 1:27-9) that God makes use of: the weak things, the foolish things, the base things, the despised things, and the things which are not, and for this purpose—that no flesh might glory in His sight—all five being just such as we should despise. He can and will use us, just when we are willing to be humble for Christ's sake, and so for six thousand years God has been teaching men; so with an ass's jawbone Samson slew his thousands (Judges 15:15), so at the blowing of rams' horns the walls of Jericho fell (Joshua 6:20). Let God work in His own way, and with His own instruments; let us all rejoice that He should, and let us too get into the position in which God can use us.

A man who has found out what his true work is—winning souls to Christ—and does it, such is the happiest man. Not the richest are these, least of all those who have just got converted for themselves, and into the Church, lost what pleasure the world could give and found none other. Job's captivity turned away when he began praying for his friends; and so will all who thus work for others shine not in heaven alone and hereafter, but here as well, and now.

I am often saddened that some pastors don't cultivate and encourage those who care about the lost. Those who do so are the life of their church. — Ray Comfort

---

But you say "I haven't got the ability." Well, God doesn't call you to do Dr. Bonar's work, or Dr. Duff's work, else He had given you their ability, their talent. The word is, "To every man his work." I have a work to do, laid out for me in the secret counsels of eternity; no other can do it. If I neglect it, it is not true that some other will do it; it will remain undone. And if, for the work laid upon us, we feel we have not the ability or talent necessary, then we have a throne of grace; and God never sends, unless that He is willing to give the strength and wisdom. The instruments He often uses may seem all unlikely, yet when did they fail? When once? And why not? Because He had fitted them out as well. He sent Moses to Egypt to deliver His people—not an eloquent, but a stuttering man. He refuses a while, at last he went; and no man once sent by God ever did break down.

We must be ready to *do little things* for God; many are willing to do the great things. I dare say hundreds would have been ready to occupy this pulpit today. How many of them would be as willing to teach a dirty class in the ragged school?

Many years ago, in between my times of teaching at a large Bible school in Dallas, TX, I would make my way to the kitchen and help the students wash and dry the dishes. I was amazed that other students heard rumors that I was helping do dishes and would show up just to stare. This shouldn't have been an unusual occurrence. All of us should be servants. — Ray Comfort

---

I remember, one afternoon I was preaching, observing a young lady from the house I was staying at, in the audience. I had heard she taught in the Sabbath school, which I knew was at the same hour; and so I asked her, after service, how she came to be there?

"Oh," said she, "my class is but five little boys, and I thought it did not matter for them." And yet among these there might have been, who knows, a Luther or a Knox, the beginning of a stream of blessing, that would have gone on widening and ever widening; and besides, one soul is worth all the kingdoms of the earth.

Another thing we want is, to be *of good courage.* Three or four times this comes out in the first chapter of Joshua; and I have observed that God never uses a man that is always looking on the dark side of things: what we do for Him let us do cheerfully, not because it is our duty—not that we should sweep away the word—but because it is our privilege. What would my wife or children say if I spoke of loving them because it was my *duty* to do so? And my mother, if I go to see her once a year, and were to say, "Mother, I am come all this way to discharge what I feel to be my duty in visiting you;" might she not rightly reply, "My son, if this is all that has brought you, you might have spared coming at all!" and go on in brokenhearted sorrow to the grave?

A London minister, a friend of mine, lately pointed out a family of seven, all of whom he was just receiving into the Church. Their story was this: going to church, he had to pass by a window, looking up at which one day, he saw a baby looking out; he smiled; the baby smiled again. Next time he passes he looks up again, smiles, and the baby smiles back. A third time going by, he looks up, and seeing the baby, throws it a kiss, which the baby returns to him. Time after time he has to pass the window, and now cannot refrain from looking up each time, and each time there are more faces to receive his smiling greeting, till by-and-by he sees the whole family grouped at the window—father, mother, and all.

The father conjectures the happy, smiling stranger must be a minister, and so, next Sunday morning, after they have received at the window the usual greeting, two of the children, ready dressed, are sent out to follow him. They enter his church, hear him preach, and carry back to their parents the report that they never heard such preaching; and what preaching could equal that of one who had so smiled on them? Soon the rest come to the church, too, and are brought in—all by a smile.

Let us not go about, hanging our heads like a bulrush; if Christ gives joy, let us live it! The whole world is in all matters for the very best thing—you always want to get the best possible thing for your money. Let us show, then, that our religion is the very best thing. Men with long, gloomy faces are never wise in the winning of souls.

<small>The Qualifications for Soul-Winning: A Sermon delivered by Dwight L. Moody in Dr. Bonar's church, Edinburgh, Scotland, 7th December, 1873.</small>

Repentance

There is a good deal of trouble among people about what repentance really is. If you ask people what it is, they will tell you "It is feeling sorry." If you ask a man if he repents, he will tell you, "Oh, yes; I generally feel sorry for my sins." That is not repentance. It is something more than feeling sorry. Repentance is turning right about and forsaking sin.

Repentance can't save us. Muslims repent. That's the basis of their hope of salvation. The same with many unsaved Catholics. They trust that their repentance is enough. But no good judge would let a devious criminal go simply because he said that he had turned from his crimes. The only thing that can save us is God's free grace; and we receive that through faith in Jesus. Salvation is by grace through faith (see Ephesians 2:8-9). The way to partake of the grace of God, is through repentance ("repentance unto life"). But it's very clear from Scripture that repentance doesn't save us. If it did, we wouldn't need a Savior. We preach free grace, through faith. Paul said of his own ministry that he spent his time "testifying both to the Jews, and also to the Greeks, repentance toward God, and faith toward our Lord Jesus Christ" (Acts 20:21, italics added). However, if someone says that they are saved, and they continue to willfully sin "after the flesh," they shouldn't have assurance of salvation. They are deceived. 1 John 3:7-9 makes that clear: "Little children, let no man deceive you: he that doeth righteousness is righteous, even as he is righteous. He that committeth sin is of the devil; for the devil sinneth from the beginning. For this purpose the Son of God was manifested, that he might destroy the works of the devil. Whosoever is born of God doth not commit sin; for his seed remaineth in him: and he cannot sin, because he is born of God." Anyone who has tasted of the grace of God continually turns from sin. His repentance is perpetual. If he doesn't turn from sin, he is a hypocrite, deceives himself, and will be one of those mentioned in Matthew 7:21-24 who cry "Lord, Lord." Our churches are filled with these false converts who think that there is a category for the "sinning" Christian. It's not in Scripture. Such a "category" comes from a lack of understanding of the reality of the spurious convert. However, if someone is a good soil hearer (genuine convert), he will put his hand to the plow and not look back, because he is "fit" for the Kingdom (see Luke 9:62). — Ray Comfort

---

You will find men sorry for their misdeeds. Cain, no doubt, was sorry, but that was not true repentance. There is no cry recorded in the Scriptures as coming from him, "O my God, O my God, forgive me." There was no repentance in his only feeling sorry. Look at Judas. There is no sign that he turned to God—no sign that he came to Christ asking forgiveness. Yet, probably, he felt sorry. He was, very likely, filled with remorse and despair; but he didn't repent. Repentance is turning to Him who loved us and gave himself for us.

Now, we read in Scripture that God deals with us as a father deals with a son. Fathers and mothers, you who have children, let me ask by way of illustration, suppose you go home, and you find that while you have been here your boy has gone to your private drawer and stolen $5 of your money. You go to him and say: "John, did you take that money?" "Yes, father, I took that money," he replies. When you hear him saying this without any apparent regret you won't forgive him. You want to get at his conscience; you know it would do him an injury to forgive him unless he confesses his wrong.

Suppose he won't do it. "Yes," he says, "I stole your money, but I don't think I've done wrong." The mother cannot, the father cannot forgive him, unless he sees he has done wrong and wants forgiveness.

That's the trouble with the sinners in Chicago. They've turned against God, broken His commandments, trampled His Law under their feet, and their sins hang upon them; until they show signs of repentance their sin will remain. But the moment they see their iniquity and come to God, forgiveness will be given them and their iniquity will be taken out of their way.

No unrepentant sinner will ever get into Heaven, unless they forsake their sin they cannot enter there. The Law of God is very plain on this point: "Except a man repent." That's the language of Scripture. And when this is so plainly set down, why is it that men fold their arms and say, "God will take me into Heaven anyway."

Make sure you listen to "Hell's Best Kept Secret" on www.livingwaters.com — Ray Comfort

Suppose a governor elected today comes into office in a few months, and he finds a great number of criminals in prison, and he goes and says: "I feel for those prisoners. They cannot stay in jail any longer." Suppose some murders have been committed, and he says: "I am tender hearted, I can't punish those men." and he opens the prison door and lets them all out. How long would that governor be in his position? These very men who are depending on the mercy of God would be the first to raise their voice against that governor. These men would say, "These murders must be punished or society will be imperiled; life will not be safe;" and yet they believe in the mercy of God whether they repent or not. My dear friends, don't go on under that delusion; it is a snare of the Devil. I tell you the Word of God is true, and it tells us "Except a man repent" there is not one ray of hope held out. May the Spirit of God open your eyes tonight and show you the truth—let it go into your hearts. Let the wicked forsake his way and the unrighteous his thoughts.

True repentance is the Holy Ghost showing sinners their sin.

It is impossible for a man to live without sinning, there are so many things, to draw away the heart and affections of men from God. I feel as if I ought to be repenting all the time.

Is there a man here who can say honestly, "I have not got a sin that I need ask forgiveness for, I haven't one thing to repent of"? Some men seem to think that God has got ten different Laws for each of those Ten Commandments, but if you have been guilty of breaking one you are guilty of breaking all. If a man steals $5 and another steals $500, the one is as guilty of theft as the other. A man who has broken one Commandment of God is as guilty as he who has broken ten. If a man doesn't feel this, and come to Him repentant and turn his face from sin toward God there is not a ray of hope. Nowhere can you find one ray from Genesis to Revelation. Don't go out of this Tabernacle saying, "I have nothing to repent."

When a man turns to God he is made a new creature—a new man. His impulses all the time are guided by love. He loves his enemies and tries to repair all wrong he has done. This is a true sign of conversion. If this sign is not apparent his conversion has never got from his head to his heart. We must be born of the Spirit, hearts must be regenerated—born again. When a man repents, and turns to the God of Heaven, then the work is deep and thorough.

Suppose I was called to New York tonight and went down to the Illinois Central Depot to catch the ten o'clock train. I go on the train, and a friend should see me and say, "You are on the wrong train for New York. You are on the Burlington train."

"Oh, no," I say, "you are wrong; I asked someone and he told me this was the right train."

"Why," this friend replies, "I've been in Chicago for twenty years, and know that you are on the wrong train," and the man talks, and at last convinces me, but I sit still, although I believe I am in the wrong train for New York, and I go on to Burlington. If you don't get off the wrong train and get on the right one you will not reach Heaven. If you have not repented, seize your baggage tonight and go to the other train.

If a man is not repentant his face is turned away from God, and the moment his face is turned toward God peace and joy follow.

When I was a little boy I remember I tried to catch my shadow. I don't know if you were ever so foolish: but I remember running after it and trying to get ahead of it. I could not see why the shadow always kept ahead of me. Once I happened to be racing with my face to the sun, and I looked over my head and saw my shadow coming back of me, and it kept behind me all the way. It is the same with the Sun of Righteousness, peace and joy will go with you while you go with your face toward Him, and these people who are getting at the back of the Sun are in darkness all the time. Turn to the light of God and the reflection will flash in your heart.

Look at that beautiful steamer Atlantic. There she is in the bay groping her way along a rocky coast. The captain don't know, as his vessel plows through that ocean, that in a few moments it will strike a rock and hundreds of those on board will perish in a watery grave. If he knew, in a minute he could strike a bell and the steamer would be turned from that rock and the people would be saved. The vessel has struck, but he knows now too late. You have time now. In five minutes, for all you and I know, you may be in eternity. God hangs a mist over our eyes as to our summons. So now God calls: Now everyone repent, and all your sins will be taken from you. I have come in the name of the Master to ask you to turn to God now. May God help you to turn and live.

Repentance: A sermon by D.L. Moody

More on The Ten Commandments

I can imagine someone saying, "I won't be weighed by that Law. I don't believe in it." Now men may cavil as much as they like about other parts of the Bible, but I have never met an honest man that found fault with the Ten Commandments. Infidels may mock the Lawgiver and reject Him who has delivered us from the curse of the Law, but they can't help admitting that the commandments are right. Renan said that they are for all nations, and will remain the commandments of God during all the centuries.

If God created this world, He must make some laws to govern it. In order to make life safe we must have good laws; there is not a country the sun shines upon that does not possess laws. Now this is God's Law. It has come from on high, and infidels and skeptics have to admit that it is pure. Legislatures nearly all over the world adopt it as the foundation of their legal systems. "The Law of the LORD is perfect, converting the soul: the testimony of the Lord is sure, making wise the simple: the statutes of the Lord are right, rejoicing the heart: the commandment of the Lord is pure, enlightening the eyes (Psalm 19:7-8). Now the question for you and me is: Are we keeping these Commandments? Have we fulfilled all the requirements of the Law? If God made us, as we know He did, He had a right to make that Law; and if we don't use it aright it would have been better for us if we had never had it, for it will condemn us. We shall be found wanting. The Law is all right, but are we right

I tell you that a man who does evil in these gospel days is far worse than that king. We live in a land of Bibles. You can get the New Testament for a nickel, and if you haven't got a nickel, you can get it for nothing. Many societies will be glad to give it to you free. We live in the full blaze of Calvary.

Let us imagine that now, while I am preaching, down come some balances from the throne of God. They are fastened to the very throne itself. It is a throne of equity, of justice. You and I must be weighed. I venture to say this would be a very solemn audience. There would be no tiring There would be no indifference. No one would be thoughtless. Some people have their own balances. A great many are making balances to be weighed in. But after all we must be weighed in God's balances, the balances of the sanctuary. It is a favorite thing with infidels to set their own standard, to measure themselves by other people. But that will not do in the Day of Judgment. Now we will use God's Law as a balance weight. When men find fault with the lives of professing Christians, it is a tribute to the Law of God.

If it were known that God himself were going to speak once again to man, what eagerness and excitement there would be! For nearly nineteen hundred years He has been silent. No inspired message has been added to the Bible for nearly nineteen hundred years. How eagerly all men would listen if God should speak once more. Yet men forget that the Bible is God's own Word, and that it is as truly His message today as when it was delivered of old. The Law that was given at Sinai has lost none of its solemnity. Time cannot wear out its authority or the fact of its authorship.

We call it the "Mosaic" Law, but it has been well said that the Commandments did not originate with Moses, nor were they done away with when the Mosaic Law was fulfilled in Christ, and many of its ceremonies and regulations abolished. We can find no trace of the existence of any lawmaking body in those early times, no parliament, or congress that built up a system of laws. It has come down to us complete and finished, and the only satisfactory account is that which tells us that God himself wrote the Commandments on tables of stone.

The conviction deepens in me with the years that the old truths of the Bible must be stated and restated in the plainest possible language.

The people must be made to understand that the Ten Commandments are still binding, and that there is a penalty attached to their violation.

Now, my friend, are you ready to be weighed by this Law of God? A great many people say that if they keep the Commandments they do not need to be forgiven and saved through Christ. But have you kept them? I will admit that if you perfectly keep the Commandments, you do not need to be saved by Christ; but is there a man in the wide world who can truly say that he has done this? Young lady, can you say: "I am ready to be weighed by the Law? Can you, young man? Will you step into the scales and be weighed one by one by the Ten Commandments? Now face these Ten Commandments honestly and prayerfully. See if your life is right, and if you are treating God fairly. God's statutes are just, are they not? If they are right, let us see if we are right. Let us get alone with God and read His Law—read it carefully and prayerfully, and ask Him to forgive us our sin and what He would have us to do.

The First Commandment Thou shalt have no other gods before Me. My friend, are you ready to be weighed against this Commandment? Have you fulfilled, or are you willing to fulfill all the requirements of this Law? Put it into one of the scales, and step into the other. Is your heart set upon God alone? Have you no other God? Do you love Him above father or mother, the wife of your bosom, your children, home or land, wealth or pleasure? If men were true to this commandment, obedience to the remaining nine would follow naturally. It is because they are unsound in this that they break the others.

Philosophers are agreed that even the most primitive races of mankind reach out beyond the world of matter to a superior Being. It is as natural for man to feel after God as it is for the ivy to feel after a support. Hunger and thirst drive man to seek for food, and there is a hunger of the soul that needs satisfying, too. Man does not need to be commanded to worship, as there is not a race so high or so low in the scale of civilization but has some kind of god. What he needs is to be directed aright. This is what the first commandment is for. Before we can worship intelligently, we must know what or whom to worship. God does not leave us in ignorance. When Paul went to Athens, he found an altar dedicated to "The Unknown God," and he proceeded to tell of Him whom we worship. When God gave the commandments to Moses, He commenced with a declaration of His own character, and demanded exclusive recognition. "I am the Lord thy God, which have brought thee out of the land of Egypt, out of the house of bondage. Thou shalt have no other gods before me" (Exodus 20:2-3).

Someone asked an Arab: "How do you know that there is a God?" "How do I know whether a man or a camel passed my tent last night?" he replied. God's footprints in nature and in our own experience are the best evidence of His existence and character.

If He created us, He certainly ought to have our homage. Is it not right that He should have the first and only place in our affections?

There are very few who in their hearts do not believe in God, but what they will not do is give Him exclusive right of way. Missionaries tell us that they could easily get converts if they did not require them to be baptized, thus publicly renouncing their idols. Many a person in our land would become a Christian if the gate was not so strait. Christianity is too strict for them. They are not ready to promise full allegiance to God alone. Many a professing Christian is a stumbling block because his worship is divided. On Sunday he worships God; on weekdays God has little or no place in his thoughts.

You don't have to go to heathen lands today to find false gods. America is full of them. Whatever you make most of is your god. Whatever you love more than God is your idol. A man may make a god of himself, of a child, of a mother, of some precious gift that God has bestowed upon him. He may forget the Giver and let his heart go out in adoration toward the gift. Many make a god of pleasure; that is what their hearts are set on. Many make a god of pleasure; that is what their hearts are set on. With many it is the god of money. But all false gods are not as gross as these. There is the atheist. He says that he does not believe in God; he denies His existence, but he can't help setting up some other god in His place. Voltaire said, "If there were no God, it would be necessary to invent one." So the atheist speaks of the Great Unknown, the First Cause, the Infinite Mind, etc. Then there is the deist. He is a man who believes in one God who caused all things; but he doesn't believe in revelation. He only accepts such truths as can be discovered by reason. He doesn't believe in Jesus Christ, or in the inspiration of the Bible. Then there is the pantheist, who says: "I believe that the whole universe is God. He is in the air, the water, the sun, the stars" the liar and the thief included.

"When I was settled in Chicago, I used to be called out to attend many funerals. I would inquire what the man was in his belief. If I found out he was an atheist, or a deist, or a pantheist, when I went to the funeral and in the presence of his friends and said one word about that man's doctrine, they would feel insulted. Why is it that in a trying hour, when they have been talking all the time against God—why is it that in the darkness of affliction they call in believers in that God to administer consolation? Why doesn't the atheist preach no hereafter, no heaven, no God in the hour of affliction?

Some years ago I went into a man's house, and when I commenced to talk about religion he turned to his daughter and said: "You had better leave the room. I want to say a few words to Mr. Moody." When she had gone, he opened a perfect torrent of infidelity upon me. "Why did you send your daughter out of the room before you said this?" I asked. "Well," he replied, "I did not think it would do her any good to hear what I said." Is his rock as our Rock? Would he have sent his daughter out if he really believed what he said?

God will not accept a divided heart. He must be absolute monarch. There is not room in your heart for two thrones. Christ said: "No man can serve two masters: for either he will hate the one, and love the other; or else he will hold to the one, and despise the other. Ye cannot serve God and mammon" (Matthew 6: 24). Mark you, He did not say, "No man shall serve ... Ye shall not serve" but "No man can serve ... Ye cannot serve." That means more than a command; it means that you cannot mix the worship of the true God with the worship of another god any more than you can mix oil and water. It cannot be done. There is not room for any other throne in the heart if Christ is there. If worldliness should come in, godliness would go out.

When God said, "I will not hold him guiltless that takes my name in vain," He meant what He said, and I don't believe anyone can be a true child of God who takes the name of God in vain. What is the grace of God for, if it is not to give me control of my temper so that I shall not lose control and bring down the curse of God upon myself? When a man is born of God, God takes the "swear" out of him. Make the fountain good, and the stream will be good. Let the heart be right; then the language will be right; the whole life will be right. But no man can serve God and keep His Law until he is born of God. There we see the necessity of the new birth. To take God's name "in vain" means either (1) lightly, without thinking, flippantly; or (2) profanely, deceitfully.

I think it is shocking to use God's name with so little reverence as is common nowadays, even among professing Christians. We are told that the Jews held it so sacred that the covenant name of God was never mentioned amongst them except once a year by the high priest on the Day of Atonement, when he went into the holy of holies. What a contrast that is to the familiar use Christians make of it in public and private worship! We are apt to rush into God's presence and rush out again without any real sense of the reverence and awe that is due Him. We forget that we are on holy ground.

Do you know how often the word "reverend" occurs in the Bible? Only once. And what is it used in connection with? God's name. Psalm 111:9: "holy and reverend is his name."

The habit of swearing is condemned by all sensible persons. It has been called 'the most gratuitous of all sin," because no one gains by it; it is "not only sinful, but useless." An old writer said that when the accusing angel, who records men's words, flies up to heaven with an oath, he blushes as he hands it in.

When a man blasphemes, he shows an utter contempt for God. I was in the army during the war, and heard men cursing and swearing. Some godly woman would pass along the ranks looking for her wounded son, and not an oath would be heard. They would not swear before their mothers, or their wives, or their sisters; they had more respect for them than they had for God!

Men often ask: "How can I keep from swearing?" I will tell you. If God puts His love into your heart, you will have no desire to curse Him.

If you give up the Sabbath the church goes; if you give up the church the home goes; and if the home goes the nation goes. That is the direction in which we are traveling.

No man enjoys idleness for any length of time. When one goes on a vacation, one does not lie around doing nothing all that time. Hard work at tennis, hunting, and other pursuits fills the hours. A healthy mind must find something to do.

Young man, young woman, how do you treat your parents? Tell me that, and I will tell you how you are going to get on in life. When I hear a young man speaking contemptuously of his grey-haired father or mother, I say he has sunk very low indeed. When I see a young man as polite as any gentleman can be when he is out in society, but who snaps at his mother and speaks unkindly to his father, I would not give the snap of my finger for his religion. If there is any man or woman on earth that ought to be treated kindly and tenderly, it is that loving mother or that loving father. If they cannot have your regard through life, what reward are they to have for all their care and anxiety? Think how they loved you and provided for you in your early days.

When I was in England, I read of a man who professed to be a Christian, who was brought before the magistrate for not supporting his aged father. He had let him go to the workhouse. My friends, I'd rather be content with a crust of bread and a drink of water than let my father or mother go to the workhouse. The idea of a professing Christian doing such a thing! God have mercy on such a godless Christianity as that! It is a withered up thing, and the breath of heaven will drive it away. Don't profess to love God and do a thing like that.

Come, now, are you ready to be weighed? If you have been dishonoring your father and mother, step into the scales and see how quickly you will be found wanting. See how quickly you will strike the beam. I don't know any man who is much lighter than one who treats his parents with contempt. Do you disobey them just as much as you dare? Do you try to deceive them? Do you call them old-fashioned, and sneer at their advice? How do you treat that venerable father and praying mother? You may be a professing Christian, but I wouldn't give much for your religion unless it gets into your life and teaches you how to live. I wouldn't give a snap of my finger for a religion that doesn't begin at home and regulate your conduct toward your parents.

I used to say: "What is the use of taking up a Law like this in an audience where, probably, there isn't a man who ever thought of, or ever will commit, murder?" But as one gets on in years, he sees many a murder that is not outright killing. I need not kill a person to be a murderer. If I get so angry that I wish a man dead, I am a murderer in God's sight. God looks at the heart and says he that hateth his brother is a murderer.

Lust is the Devil's counterfeit of love. There is nothing more beautiful on earth than a pure love, and there is nothing so blighting as lust. I do not know of a quicker, shorter way down to hell than by adultery and the kindred sins condemned by this commandment. The Bible says that with the heart man believeth unto righteousness, but "whoredom and wine and new wine take away the heart" (Hosea 4: 11). Lust will drive all natural affection out of a man's heart. For the sake of some vile harlot he will trample on the feelings and entreaties of a sainted mother and beautiful wife and godly sister.

Young man, are you leading an impure life? Suppose God's scales should drop down before you, what would you do? Are you fit for the kingdom of heaven? May God show us what a fearful sin it is! The idea of making light of it! I do not know of any sin that will make a man run down to ruin more quickly. I am appalled when I think of what is going on in the world; of so many young men living impure lives, and talking about the virtue of women as if it didn't amount to anything. This sin is coming in upon us like a hood at the present day. In every city there is an army of prostitutes. Young men by hundreds are being utterly ruined by this accursed sin.

Young man, young woman, are you guilty, even in thought? Bear in mind what Christ said: "Ye have heard that it was said by them of old time, Thou shalt not commit adultery:

but I say unto you, That whosoever looketh on a woman to lust after her has committed adultery with her already in his heart" (Matthew 5: 27-28).

How many would repent but that they are tied hand and foot, and some vile harlot whose feet are fastened in hell, clings to him and says: "If you give me up, I will expose you!" Can you step on the scales and take that harlot with you? If you are guilty of this awful sin, escape for your life. Hear God's voice while there is yet time. Confess your sin to Him. Ask Him to snap the fetters that bind you. Ask Him to give you victory over your passions. If your right eye offends, pluck it out. If your right hand offends, cut it off. Shake yourself like Samson, and say: "By the grace of God I will not go down to an adulterer's grave."

There is hope for you, adulterer. There is hope for you, adulteress. God will not turn you away if you truly repent. No matter how low down in vice and misery you may have sunk, you may be washed, you may be sanctified, you may be justified in the name of the Lord Jesus, and by the Spirit of our God. Remember what Christ said to that woman which was a sinner, "Thy sins are forgiven ... thy faith hath saved thee; go in peace" (Luke 7:47-50); and to that woman that was taken in adultery, "Go, and sin no more" (John 8:11).

The story is told that one of Queen Victoria's diamonds valued at six-hundred thousand dollars was stolen from a jeweler's window, to whom it had been given to set. A few months afterward a miserable man died a miserable death in a poor lodging house. In his pocket was found the diamond and a letter telling how he had not dared to sell it lest it lead to his discovery and imprisonment. It never brought him anything but anxiety and pain. Everything you steal is a curse to you in that way. The sin overreaches itself. A man who takes money that does not belong to him never gets any lasting comfort. He has no real pleasure, for he has a guilty conscience.

We have got nowadays so that we divide lies into white lies and black lies, society lies, business lies, etc. The Word of God knows no such letting down of the standard. A lie is a lie, no matter what are the circumstances under which it is uttered, or by whom.

The greatest dupe the Devil has in the world is the hypocrite; but the next greatest is the covetous man, "for a man's life consisteth not in the abundance of the things which he possesseth" (Luke 12:15).

These Ten Commandments are not ten different Laws; they are one law. If I am being held up in the air by a chain with ten links and I break one of them, down I come, just as surely as if I break the whole ten. If I am forbidden to go out of an enclosure, it makes no difference at what point I break through the fence. "Whosoever shall keep the whole Law, and yet offend in one point, he is guilty of all" (James 2:10). The golden chain of obedience is broken if one link is missing.

For fifteen hundred years man was under the Law, and no one was equal to it. Christ came and showed that the commandments went beyond the mere letter; and can anyone since say that he has been able to keep them in his own strength? As the plummet is held up, we see how much we are out of the perpendicular. As we measure ourselves by that holy standard, we find how much we are lacking. As a child said, when reproved by her mother and told that she ought to do right: "How can I do right when there is no right in me?" "All have sinned and come short of the glory of God" (Romans 3:23), "There is none righteous, no, not one" (Romans 3:10).

The moral man is as guilty as the rest. His morality cannot save him. "Except ye repent, ye shall all likewise perish" (Luke 13:3, 5). "Except ye be converted, and become as little children, ye shall not enter into the kingdom of heaven" (Matthew 18:3). I have often heard good people say that our meetings were doing good, they were reaching the drunkards, and gamblers, and harlots; but they never realized that they needed the grace of God for themselves.

Nicodemus was probably one of the most moral men of his day. He was a teacher of the Law. Yet Christ said to him: "Except a man be born again, he cannot see the kingdom of God." It is much easier to reach thieves and drunkards and vagabonds than self-righteous Pharisees. You do not have to preach to those men for weeks and months to convince them that they are sinners. When a man learns that he has need of God and that he is a sinner, it is very easy to reach him. But the self-righteous Pharisee needs salvation as much as any drunkard that walks the streets.

I read of a minister traveling in the South who obtained permission to preach in the local jail. A son of his host went with him. On the way back the young man who was not a Christian, said to the minister: "I hope some of the convicts were impressed. Such a sermon as that ought to do them good."

"Did it do you good?" the minister asked. "Oh, you were preaching to the convicts," the young man answered. The minister shook his head and said: "I preached Christ, and you need Him as much as they." If you do not repent of your sins and ask Him for mercy, there is no hope for you.

I can imagine that you are saying to yourself, "If we are to be judged by these Laws, how are we going to be saved? Nearly every one of them has been broken by us—in spirit, if not in letter."

I almost hear you say: "I wonder if Mr. Moody is ready to be weighed. Would he like to put those tests to himself?" With all humility I reply that if God commanded me to step into the scales now, I am ready. "What!" you say, "haven't you broken the Law?"

Yes, I have. I was a sinner before God, the same as you; but forty years ago I pled guilty at His bar. I cried for mercy, and He forgave me. If I step into the scales, the Son of God has promised to be with me. I would not dare to step in without Him. If I did, how quickly the scales would fly up! Christ kept the Law. If He had ever broken it, He would have to die for himself; but because He was a Lamb without spot or blemish, His atoning death is efficacious for you and me. He had no sin of His own to atone for, and so God accepted His sacrifice. Christ is the end of the Law for righteousness to everyone that believeth. We are righteous in God's sight, because the righteousness of God which is by faith in Jesus Christ is unto all and upon all them that believe. If we had to live forever with our sins in the handwriting of God on the wall, it would be hell on Earth. But thank God for the Gospel we preach! If we repent, our sins will all be blotted out. "You, being dead in your sins ... hath he quickened together with him, having forgiven you all trespasses; blotting out the handwriting of ordinances that was against us, which was contrary to us, and took it out of the way, nailing it to his Cross" (Colossians 2:13-14)." D.L. Moody

More on The Ten Commandments by D.L. Moody

Christ All in All

"Whosoever will, let him take the water of life freely." That is the message for the sinner. I am sent to preach the gospel to all.

Supposing I saw a man tumble into a river, and I were to jump in and rescue him, I should be a savior to him—I should have saved him. But when I brought the man ashore, I should probably leave him, and do nothing further. But the Lord does more. He not only saves us, but He redeems us—that is, buys us back. He ransoms us from the power of sin, as if I should promise to watch over that rescued man for ever, and see that he did not again fall into the water. The Lord not only saves us from spiritual death, but He redeems us for ever that death can never touch us.

In Isaiah 49:24, we read: "Shall the prey be taken from the mighty, or the Lawful captive delivered? But thus saith the Lord, Even the captives of the mighty shall be taken away, and the prey of the terrible shall be delivered: for I will contend with him that contendeth with thee, and I will save thy children."

I will save him; I will deliver him. The children of Israel were saved from the cruel bondage of Egypt, they were led out of the land of Goshen; but still they were not fully delivered. The great host of the Egyptians was thundering behind them. It was not till they had passed safely through the Red Sea, which closing behind them, swallowed up the host of the enemy. It was not till then that they were free, that they were delivered. And similarly in our times of danger we shall find it to be true of Christ, "He delivered my soul;" and again in Job 33:24-28, "Then He is gracious unto him, and saith, Deliver him from going down to the pit: I have found a ransom. His flesh shall be fresher than a child's: he shall return to the days of his youth: he shall pray unto God, and He will be favorable unto him: and he shall see His face with joy: for He will render unto man His righteousness. He will deliver his soul from going into the pit, and his life shall see the light."

Here we have the saving, the redeeming, the deliverance from the pit. Man is fallen into the deep pit, he is kept there a lawful captive by one who is mighty. If he is to be brought back from the darkness of the pit to see the light, then we must have a ransom. Here God comes forward, and says, "I have found a ransom." Christ is the ransom, and He will deliver us. Sound out the cry, "Christ is our deliverer." He is mighty to save, He is able to deliver.

"Bread of heaven, Feed me till I want no more." Yes, that is the true prayer of the bewildered sinner. God is able, and still more, He is willing, to lead us, and to feed us. "Thou gavest them bread from heaven for their hunger, and broughtest forth water for them out of the rock for their thirst" (Nehemiah 9:15).

May God help His own people to shine brightly, to flash out of darkness, that men may take knowledge of us that we have been with Jesus. But remember, the world hates the light. Christ was the light of the world, and the world sought to extinguish it at Calvary. Now He has left His people to shine. "Ye are the light of the world." He has left us here to shine. He means us to be "living epistles, known and read of all men." The world is certain to watch, and to read you and me. If we are inconsistent, then you may be sure the world will take occasion to stumble at us. The world finds plenty of difficulties on the way; let us see that we Christians do not add more stumbling blocks by our un-Christlike walk. God help us to keep our lights burning clear and brilliant!

Out West a friend of mine was walking along one of the streets one dark night, and saw approaching him a man with a lantern. As he came up close to him he noticed by the bright light that the man had no eyes. He went past, but the thought struck him, "Surely that man is blind." He turned round, and said, "My friend, are you not blind?" "Yes." "Then what have you got the lantern for?" "I carry the lantern that people may not stumble over me, of course," said the blind man. Let us take a lesson from that blind man, and hold up our light, burning with the clear radiance of heaven, that men may not stumble over us.

I remember during the American war I was in a prayer meeting. We were all very dark and gloomy. Things had been going against us for some time. At last an old man got up, and said, "What is the matter with us, that we are downhearted and sad? It is simply our lack of faith. Moses, Joshua, and David were men strong in faith. They believed, and therefore God honored them. Whence comes our want of faith? God is not dead. He is as powerful, as willing, to help today as ever He was. Why, then, are we not full of faith in Him? It is God dishonoring to forget that He still has power, although our armies are defeated, and all seems dark and gloomy.

I will tell you what happened to me some time ago when I was out West. I wanted to reach the summit of one of the Western mountains. I had been told that sunrise was very beautiful when seen from the summit. We got up to the halfway house one afternoon, where we were to rest till midnight, and then set out for the top. Soon a little party of us started with a good guide. Before a great while it began to rain, and then it became a regular storm of thunder and lightning. I thought there was little use in going on, and said to the guide, "Guess we'd better turn back; we won't see anything this morning, with all these clouds."

"Oh," said the guide, "I expect we'll soon get through these clouds, and get above them, and then we'll have a glorious view."

So we went on, whilst the thunders were rumbling right about our ears. But soon we began to get above the thundercloud; the air was quite clear, and when the sun rose we had a splendid view of his rays as they tinged the hilltops; and then, as the glorious sunshine began to break on where we stood, we could see the dark cloud far beneath our mountain height. That's what God's people want—to get into the clear air above the stormy clouds, and to CLIMB HIGHER away up to the mountain peak. There you'll catch the first rays from the Sun of Righteousness far above the clouds and mists.

Some of you may be in great darkness and gloom; but fear not, climb higher, get nearer to the Master, and soon you'll catch His bright rays on your own soul, and they will sprinkle back upon others.

What a wonderful thing to have a teacher sent from heaven. "If any man lack wisdom, let him ask of God, that giveth to all men liberally, and upbraideth not; and it shall be given him" (James 1:5).

"If any lack wisdom": I am afraid there are a great many of us who lack wisdom, and even the best of us at times will be in perplexity. There are moments in the life of us all when we seem in a fix; we just stand still, and say, "What shall I do? I don't know what is the best way." Oh, leave it with God, He will himself be our teacher! "Come unto me, all ye that labor and are heavy laden, and I will give you rest. Take my yoke upon you, and learn of me." Here is a wonderful teacher. He has had a school for many thousand years; He has had the best men in His school; but still there's room for another scholar there. His college is not too full yet, and the teacher is the One sent from heaven.

Anxious sinner, seek the good teacher, as Nicodemus did: "Master, we know thou art a teacher sent from God." If you seek Him thus He will direct you. He will keep you, and lead you into green pastures and by the still waters. I met a woman the other day who was full of infidel doubts and fancies. She could not believe. Reading for some time infidel works had thrown a dark and gloomy pall over her mind. It made me sad to see her in such a case. Some of you may be like her. I wish you would take Christ as your teacher, and then all darkness would flee away. Christ is able to teach us. See how He taught the disciples. He never wearied of their learning from Him. So He will teach us if we will only listen to Him.

If time permitted, I should like to take up the subject of Christ as our Justification, our Wisdom, our Righteousness, the Friend that sticketh closer than a brother; but it would take a whole eternity to tell what Christ is to His people and what He does for them. I remember when I was preaching on this subject in Scotland; after I was done, I said to a man that I was sorry I could not finish the subject for want of time. "Finish the subject?" said the Scotchman, "Why, that would require all eternity, and even then it would not be complete; it will be the occupation of heaven."

On one occasion … a woman came forward and said, "Oh, Mr. Moody, it's all very well for you to talk like that, about a light heart. But you are a young man, and if you had a heavy burden like me you would talk differently. I could not talk in that way, my burden is too great."

I replied, "But it's not too great for Jesus." "Oh," she said, "I cannot cast it on Him." "Why not? surely it is not too great for Him. It is not that He is feeble. But it is because you will not leave it to Him. You're like many others. They will not leave it with Him. They go about hugging their burden, and yet crying out against it. What the Lord wants is, you to leave it with Him, to let Him carry it for you. Then you will have a light heart, sorrow will flee away, and there will be no more sighing. What is your burden, my friend, that you cannot leave with Christ?"

She replied, "I have a son who is a wanderer on the face of the earth. None but God knows where he is." "Cannot Christ find him, and bring him back?" "I suppose He can." "Then go and tell Jesus, and ask Him to forgive you for doubting His power and willingness; you have no right to mistrust Him." She went away much comforted, and I believe she ultimately had her wandering boy restored to her!

Christ All in All: A sermon by D.L. Moody

A Mother's Prayer Answered

A faithful father and mother in our country—whose eldest son had gone to Chicago to a situation—[and] a neighbor of theirs [that] was in the city on some business, met the young man reeling along the streets drunk. He thought, "How am I to tell his parents?"

When he returned to his village, he went and called out the father, and told him. It was a terrible blow to that father, but he said nothing to the mother till the little ones had all gone to rest, the servants had retired, and all was quiet in that little farm on the Western prairies. They drew up their chairs to the little drawing room table, and then he told her the sad news. "Our boy has been seen drunk on the streets of Chicago—drunk." Ah, that mother was sorely hurt; they did not sleep much that night, but spent the hours in fervent prayers for their boy.

About daybreak the mother felt an inward conviction that all would be well. She told the father she had cast it on the Lord, had left her son with Jesus, and she felt He would save him. One week from that time the young man left Chicago, took a journey of three hundred miles into the country, and when he reached his home, he walked in and said, "Mother, I've come home to ask you to pray for me." Ah, her prayer had reached heaven; she had cast her burden on Jesus, and He had borne it for her. He took the burden, presented her prayer sprinkled with the atoning blood, and got it answered. In two days that young man returned to Chicago rejoicing in the Savior.

What a wonderful thing it is to have Christ as our burden bearer! How easy, how light do our cares become when cast upon Him!

Does God Answer Prayer?

We cannot but notice that every man of God spoken of in the Bible was a man of *prayer*. You have therefore very good authority and encouragement for asking God to hear your prayers, and for praying on behalf of others, as we are daily requested to do. Many are surprised at these requests. But many mothers and fathers are rejoicing that they sent them in. The prayers offered up here have been answered, and their children have been saved.

Last night I was more confirmed in my views regarding the power of *prayer* than ever. "This is all excitement," some say; "it is got up by earnest appeals that work on the feelings of people, and move their impulses, making them uneasy and anxious."

Now, for example, there was nothing said last night to speak of, and I never was more disgusted with myself than I was on Sunday night. It seemed as if I could not preach the Gospel, as if my tongue would not speak. But still the number of inquirers was extraordinary. Last night, when there was no speaking at all, and when I just came in and asked that any inquirers might follow me into the moderator's room, taking a few with me, and expecting to come in and ask out a few more when I had seen these, the number was so great that came out without solicitation that I did not need to return. I saw over a hundred inquirers last night, and there were from fifty to seventy that I had to close the door on, being unable to see them.

A great many who have not been at the meetings at all, have been converted in their own homes. God is working, not we. Oh! that we would keep ourselves down in the dust, and every one of us get out of the way, and let God work. It would be so easy for Him to go into every dwelling in Edinburgh, and convict and convert ten thousand souls.

Look at the 6th verse of the 4th chapter of Philippians. "Be careful for nothing, but in everything"—mark that—"by prayer and supplication, with thanksgiving, let your requests be made known unto God." He doesn't say He will answer all, but He says, "And the peace of God, which passeth all understanding, shall keep your hearts and minds through Jesus Christ." He tells us to make our wants known; to make our requests known to Him by prayer and supplication. It is right to come and make our requests known. He has told us to come and pray for the conversion of souls.

Turn to the 20th chapter of 2nd Chronicles. There we read that the Moabites, the Ammonites, and others coming against Jehoshaphat, he was afraid, "and set himself to seek the Lord," and that afterwards Judah "gathered themselves together to ask help of the Lord." That is what we want—to seek the Lord not only here in the public assembly, but alone. If you have got an unconverted friend and are anxious that he should be saved, go and tell it privately to Jesus, and if a blessing does not come, like Jehoshaphat, spend a few days in fasting, and prayer, and humiliation.

When I go into the streets and see the terrible wickedness, and blasphemy, and drunkenness that is in them, it seems dark, but I look up and think that God can repel those dark waves of sin and iniquity. Let us pray that God will bless this land of Scotland, bless and save all the people in it. It would be a great thing for us, but very little for God. May God give us faith!

Does God Answer Prayer? A sermon by D.L. Moody

Enduement For Service

When the disciples were about to begin their great work, our Lord said: "Ye shall receive power, after that the Holy Ghost is come upon you." How many, do you suppose, would have been converted on the day of Pentecost if Peter had gone and preached without this power? Not one. The disciples were commissioned to go and preach, but they were to wait till they were recommissioned and endued with power by the Holy Ghost. "Ye shall receive power, after that the Holy Ghost is come upon you: and ye shall be witnesses unto Me, both in Jerusalem, and in all Judea, and in Samaria, and unto the uttermost part of the earth." How quickly this whole world would be reached if we were just looking to God for this same Apostolic power!

There was a time when I thought the raising of Lazarus was the greatest work ever done on this earth. But I think the conversion of those 3,000 Jews on the day of Pentecost was more wonderful still. Those hard-hearted Jews were full of hatred and unbelief; many, no doubt, were the same men who murdered Christ. And yet they were swept down by the mighty power of the Spirit. We have got the same obstacles to contend with as the Apostles had. Our Gospel that we are preaching is a supernatural Gospel, and we have got to have supernatural power to preach it.

Notice that those who are filled with the Holy Ghost immediately begin to testify of Jesus Christ. Elisabeth, when visited by the Virgin, was "filled with the Holy Ghost," and spoke of the coming Lord. Zacharias also was "filled with the Holy Ghost," and quoted Scripture in reference to the Messiah. Stephen was "filled with the Spirit," and received such unction that the men of the synagogue "were not able to resist the wisdom and the spirit by which he spake." He was able to stand before the whole Sanhedrim, and the power of God was on him in a wonderful degree while he testified of Christ.

When Peter was "filled with the Spirit" he went out to preach Christ—he couldn't help it. All through the New Testament we are told that the Apostles were again and again filled with the Spirit. And as they preached "much people were added to the church." That always follows. There will be conversions breaking out in all the churches if we are filled with the Spirit. Let us pray that we may receive power for service. Let us not be satisfied with only the power by which we are "sealed unto the day of redemption;" but let us pray that we may be baptized with that power from on high by which we can do great things for the Master.

It is important to know whether the work we are doing is the work God would have us do. I remember that one time when Dr. Kirk came to Chicago, his old power came back upon him, and he just shook that city as I had never seen it shaken. I suppose if he had stayed, there would have been thousands and thousands converted. The Mayor of the city and the leading men all came to hear him, and they said: "If we could have that kind of preaching we would be glad to hear it." But he went back to his pastoral work. I believe that man was meant for an evangelist; yet he went back to visit the widow and the fatherless. That was an important work, but others could have done it. Some men are gifted one way and some another. One man has got gifts as a pastor, and another has got gifts as an evangelist, while another is specially qualified to stir up Christians. Let every one ask, "Am I in the right place? Am I where God wants me to be?" If we would do that, it might break up a good many pastorates. Are you ready—ready to cut the tie?

When I was in Chicago I used to take a circuit out in the country, and preach during the week evenings; but I think I made a great mistake in binding myself too closely to my regular work. There was time after time when there would be a hundred inquirers in the country, and yet I would hurry away so as to preach in my own place in the city on Sunday night, and then perhaps only find myself beating against the air. Let us be ready to go anywhere—to go wherever the Master calls.

Just say: "Here I am, Lord. Send me where you please—only give me souls. Give me power to win souls for Jesus Christ." When that is the uppermost thought in our hearts He won't disappoint us. "He that spared not His own Son, but delivered Him up for us all, how shall He not with Him also freely give us all things." If He gave us His Son, will He withhold the Spirit? "Herein is My Father glorified, that ye bear much fruit."

Are you toiling all night and catching nothing? Cast the net on the right side. Come, my friend, are you ready to go anywhere? Can you say: "Lord, send me to whom you will—only send me. Let that power come upon me, that I may win souls for Jesus Christ?" May we have no will but God's sweet will. Oh, that our wills may be swallowed up in God's will.

Enduement For Service: A sermon by D.L. Moody

Tomorrow May Be Too Late

I have learned that when anyone becomes in earnest about his soul's salvation and he begins to seek God, it does not take long for an anxious sinner to meet an anxious Saviour. "Ye shall seek me, and find me, when ye shall search for me with all your heart" (Jeremiah 29:13). Those who seek for Him with all their hearts, find Christ.

I believe the reason why so few find Christ is that they do not search for Him with all their hearts; they are not terribly in earnest about their souls' salvation.

Everything God has done proves that He is in earnest about the salvation of men's souls. He has proved it by giving His only Son to die for us. The Son of God was in earnest when He died. What is Calvary but a proof of that? And the Lord wants us to be in earnest when it comes to this great question of the soul's salvation. I never saw men seeking Him with all their hearts but they soon found Him.

It was quite refreshing one night to find in the inquiry room a young man who thought he was not worth saving, he was so vile and wicked. There was hope for him because he was so desperately in earnest about his soul. He thought he was worthless. He had a sight of himself in God's looking glass and had a very poor opinion of himself. One can always tell when a man is a great way from God, for he is always talking about himself, and how good he is. But the moment he sees God by the eye of faith, he is down on his knees, and, like Job, he cries, "Behold, I am vile." All his goodness flees away.

When men earnestly seek the Lord and are in earnest about their salvation, they will soon find Christ. You do not need to go up to the heights to bring Him down, or down to the depths to bring Him up, or go off to some distant city to find Him. This day He is near to every one of us.

I once heard someone in the inquiry room telling a young person to go home and seek Christ in his closet. I would not dare tell anyone to do that. He might be dead before he got home. If I read my Bible correctly, the man who preaches the Gospel will not tell me to seek Christ tomorrow or an hour hence, but now. He is near to every one of us this minute to save.

Suppose I should say I have lost a very valuable diamond here worth $100,000. I had it in my pocket when I came into the hall, and when I was done preaching, it was not in my pocket but in the hall somewhere. Suppose I should say that anyone who finds it could have it. How earnest you would all become! You would not get very much of my sermon for thinking of the diamond. I do not believe the police could get you out of this hall. The idea of finding a diamond worth $100,000! If I could only find it, it would lift me out of poverty at once, and I would be independent for the rest of my days! Oh, how soon everybody would become terribly in earnest! I would to God I could get men to seek for Christ in the same way. I have something worth more than a diamond to offer you. Is not salvation—eternal life—worth more than all the diamonds in the world?

People seem to forget that there is no door out of Hell. If they enter there, they must remain there age after age. Millions on millions of years will roll on, but there is no door, no escape out of Hell.

People talk about our being earnest and fanatical—about our being on fire. Would to God the church were on fire! This world would soon shake to its foundation. May God wake up a slumbering church! What we want you to do is not to shout "amen" and clap your hands. The deepest and quietest waters very often run swiftest. We want you to go right to work; there will be a chance for you to shout by and by. Go and speak to your neighbor and tell him of Christ and Heaven. You need not go far before you will find someone passing down to the darkness of eternal death. Haste to his rescue!

We want you to go right to work; there will be a chance for you to shout by and by. Go and speak to your neighbor and tell him of Christ and Heaven. You need not go far before you will find someone passing down to the darkness of eternal death. Haste to his rescue! What we want to see is people really wishing to become Christians, those who are in dead earnest about it. The idea of hearing one say in answer to the question, "Do you want to become a Christian?" "Well, I would not mind"! My friend, you will never get into the Kingdom of God until you change your language. Men should be crying from the depths of their hearts, "I want to be saved!"

When men seek Christ as they do wealth, they will soon find Him. To be sure, the world will raise a cry that they are excited. Let cotton go up ten or fifteen percent before tomorrow morning, and you will see how quickly the merchants will get excited! And the papers won't cry it down either. They say it is healthy excitement; commerce is getting on. But when you begin to get excited about your soul and are in earnest, then they raise the cry, "Oh, they are getting excited; most unhealthy state of things." Yet they don't talk nor write about men hastening down to death by the thousands.

There is the poor drunkard—look at him! Hear the piercing cry going up to Heaven? Yet the Church of God slumbers and sleeps. Here and there is an inquirer, yet they go into the inquiry room as if they were half asleep. When will men seek for Christ as they seek for wealth, or as they seek for honor?

There is a story told of a vessel that was wrecked and was going down at sea. There were not enough lifeboats to take all on board. When the vessel went down, some of the lifeboats were near the vessel. A man swam from the wreck to one of the boats, but they had no room to take him on. When they refused, he seized hold of the boat with his right hand, but they took a sword and cut off his fingers. When he had lost the fingers of his right hand, the man was so earnest to save his life that he seized the boat with his left hand. They cut off the fingers of that hand too. Then the man swam up and seized the boat with his teeth. Now they had compassion on him and relented. They could not cut off his head, so they took him in, and the man's life was saved. Why? Because he was in earnest. Why not seek your soul's salvation as that man sought to save his life?

Will there ever be a better time for the old man whose locks are growing gray, whose eyes are growing dim, and who is hastening to the grave? Is not this the very best time for him? "Seek ye the Lord while he may be found."

There is a man in the middle of life. Is this not the best time for him to seek the Kingdom of God? Will he ever have a better opportunity? Will Christ ever be more willing to save than now? He says, "Come; for all things are now ready"—not "going to be," but "are now ready."

There is a young man. My friend, is it not the best time for you to seek the Kingdom of God? Seek the Lord; you can find Him now. Can you say that you will find Him tomorrow? Young man, you know not what tomorrow may bring forth. Do you know that every time the clock ticks, a soul passes away? Is not this the best time for you to seek the Kingdom of God? My boy, the Lord wants you. Seek first the Kingdom of God, and seek Him while He may be found.

At Dublin a young man found Christ. He went home and lived so godly and so Christlike a life that two of his brothers could not understand what had wrought the change in him. They left Dublin and followed us to Sheffield, and there found Christ. They were in earnest. But, thanks be to God, Christ can be found now. I firmly believe every reader can find Christ now, if you will seek for Him with all your heart. He says, "Call upon me."

Men are pretty near the kingdom of God when they do not see anything good in themselves.

At the Fulton Street prayer meeting a man came in, and this was his story. He had a mother who prayed for him—he was a wild, reckless prodigal. Some time after his mother's death he began to be troubled. He thought he ought to get into new company and leave his old companions, so he said he would go and join a secret society. He thought he would join the Odd Fellows. They made inquiry about him, and when they found he was a drunken sailor, they blackballed him. They would not have him. He went to the Freemasons. He had nobody to recommend him. When they inquired and found there was no good in his character, they blackballed him. They didn't want him. One day someone handed him a little notice in the street about the prayer meeting. He went. He heard that Christ had come to save sinners. He believed Him; he took Him at His word; and, in reporting the matter, he said he "came to Christ without a character, and Christ hadn't blackballed him."

Are you without a character, with nobody to say a good word for you? I bring you good news. Call on the Son of God, and He will hear you.

Let us be in earnest about the salvation of our children and friends. Warn that young lady. Yes, Mother, speak to that daughter. Father, speak to that child. Wife, speak to your unconverted husband. Husband, speak to your unconverted wife. Do not let anyone say, "Nobody cares for my soul." I never saw parents burdened for their children but that the children soon became anxious to be saved.

Every true friend, if you could get his advice, would tell you to be saved now. Ask your minister, "Had I better seek the Kingdom of God now?" What will he tell you? "By all means, don't put it off another minute." Ask your godly, praying mother, "Is it best to seek the Kingdom of God now?" Will she say, "Put it off one week, or a month"? There is not a Christian mother in this land who would say that. I doubt if there is even an unconverted mother whose advice would be to put off becoming a Christian. Ask that praying sister of yours, that praying brother, any friend you have, whether it is not the very best thing you can do. And then cry to Heaven and ask Him who is sitting at the right hand of God, and who loves you more than your father or your mother or anyone on Earth—who loves you so much that He gave Himself for you—ask Him what He will have you do, and hear His voice from the throne, "Seek ye first the Kingdom of God." And then shout down to the infernal regions, and ask those down there. What will they say? "Send someone to my father's house, for I have five brethren, that he may testify unto them, lest they also come into this place." Heaven, Earth, and Hell unite in this one thing: "Seek ye first the Kingdom of God." Don't put it off. Call upon Him while He is near. And if you call upon Him in earnest, He will hear that call

I have no doubt that those who would not pray when the ark was being built, prayed when the Flood came; but their prayer was not answered. I have no doubt that when Lot went out of Sodom, Sodom cried to God; but it was too late, and God's judgment swept them from the earth. My friend, it is not too late now, but it may be at twelve o'clock tonight. I cannot find any place in the Bible where it says you may call tomorrow. I am not justified in saying that. "Behold, NOW is the accepted time; behold, NOW is the day of salvation."

Tomorrow May Be Too Late: A sermon by D.L. Moody

Heaven — Its Hope

Men's ideas differ about the extent that human skill can go; but the reason why we believe the Bible is inspired, is so simple that the humblest child of God can comprehend it. If the proof of its divine origin lay in its wisdom alone, a simple and uneducated man might not be able to believe it. We believe it is inspired, because there is nothing in it that could not have come from God. God is wise, and God is good. There is nothing in the Bible that is not wise, and there is nothing in it that is not good.

If the Bible had anything in it that was opposed to reason, or to our sense of right, then, perhaps, we might think that it was like all the books in the world that are written merely by men. Books that are just human books—like merely human lives—have in them a great deal that is foolish and a great deal that is wrong. The life of Christ alone was perfect, being both human and divine. Not one of the other volumes, like the Koran, that claim divinity of origin, agree with common sense. There is nothing at all in the Bible that does not conform to common sense. What it tells us about the world having been destroyed by a deluge, and Noah and his family alone being saved, is no more wonderful than what is being taught in the schools—that all of the earth we see now, and everything upon it came out of a ball of fire. It is a great deal easier to believe that man was made after the image of God than it is to believe, as some young men and women are being taught now, that he was once a monkey.

What the Bible tells about Heaven is not half so strategic as what Professor Proctor tells about the hosts of stars that are beyond the range of any telescope, yet people very often think that science is all fact, and that religion is only fancy. A great many persons who think that Jupiter and many more of the stars around us are inhabited, cannot bring themselves to believe that there is a life beyond this earth for immortal souls. The true Christian puts faith before reason, and believes that reason always goes wrong when faith is set aside. If people would but read their Bibles more, and study what there is to be found there about Heaven, they would not be as worldly minded as they are. They would not have their hearts set upon things down here, but would seek the imperishable things above.

It seems perfectly reasonable that God should have given us a glimpse of the future, for we are constantly losing some of our friends by death, and the first thought that comes to us is, "Where have they gone?" When a loved one is taken away from us, how that thought comes up before us! How we wonder if we will ever see them again, and where and when it will be! Then it is that we turn to this blessed Book, for there is no other book in all the world that can give us the slightest comfort; no other book that can tell us where the loved ones have gone.

There are men who say that there is no Heaven. I was once talking with a man who said he thought there was nothing to justify us in believing in any other Heaven than we know here on Earth. If this is Heaven, it is a very strange one—this world of sickness, and sorrow, and sin. I pity from the depths of my heart the man or woman who has that idea. This world that so many think is Heaven, is the home of sin, a hospital of sorrow, a place that has nothing in it to satisfy the soul. Men go all over it and then want to get out of it. The more one sees of the world the less they think of it. People soon grow tired of the best pleasures it has to offer. Some one has said that the world is a stormy sea, whose every wave is strewed with the wrecks of mortals that perish in it. Every time we breathe, someone is dying. We all know that we are going to stay here but a very little while. Our life is but a vapor. It is just a mere shadow. We meet one another, as someone has said, salute one another, and pass on and are gone.

The longest time man has to live, has no more proportion to eternity than a drop of dew has to the ocean.

I do not think that it is wrong for us to think and talk about Heaven. I would like to locate Heaven and find out all I can about it. I expect to live there through all eternity. If I was going to dwell in any place in this country, if I was going to make it my home, I would want to inquire about the place, about its climate, about the neighbors I would have, and about everything in fact, that I could learn concerning it. If any of you were going to emigrate, that would be the way you would feel.

Well, we are all going to emigrate in a very little while to a country that is very far away. We are going to spend eternity in another world—a grand and glorious world where God reigns. Is it right and natural, then, that we should look and listen and try to find out who is already there, and what is the route to take?

Soon after I was converted, an infidel asked me one day why I looked up when I prayed. He said that Heaven was no more above as than below us; that Heaven was everywhere. Well, I was greatly bewildered, and the next time I prayed, it seemed almost as if I was praying into the air. Since then I have become better acquainted with the Bible, and I have come to see that Heaven is above us; that it is upward and not downward. The Spirit of God is everywhere, but God is in Heaven, and Heaven is above our heads. It does not matter what part of the globe we may stand upon, Heaven, is above us.

Look at the cities of the past. There is Babylon. It was founded by a woman named Semiramis, who had two millions of men at work for years building it. It is nothing but dust now. Nearly a thousand years ago, some historian wrote that the ruins of Nebuchadnezzar's palace were still standing, but men were afraid to go near them because they were full of scorpions and snakes. That's the sort of ruin that greatness often comes to in our own day.

When I was in Dublin, they were telling me about a father who had lost a little boy, and he had not thought about the future, he bad been so entirely taken up with this world and its affairs; but when that little boy—his only child—died, that father's heart was broken, and every night when he got home from work, they would find him with his tallow candle and his Bible in his room. He was hunting up all that he could find there about Heaven. Someone asked him what he was doing, and he said he was trying to find out where his child had gone, and I think he was a reasonable man.

My friends, let us believe this good old Book, that Heaven is not a myth, and let us be prepared to follow the dear ones who have gone before. There, and there alone, can we find the peace we seek for.

What has been, and is now, one of the strongest feelings in the human heart? Is it not to find some better place, some lovelier spot, than we have now? It is for this that men are seeking everywhere; and yet, they can have it, if they will; but instead of looking down, they must look up to find it. As men grow in knowledge, they vie with each other more and more to make their homes attractive, but the brightest home on Earth is but an empty barn compared with the mansions that are in the skies.

Dwight L. Moody

You know, when a man is going up in a balloon, he takes in sand as a ballast, and when he wants to mount a little higher, he throws out a little of the ballast, and then he will mount a little higher; he throws out a little more ballast, and he mounts still higher; and the higher he gets the more he throws out, and so the nearer we get to God the more we have to throw out of the things of this world. Let go of them; do not let us first set our hearts and affections on them, but do what the Master tells us: Lay up for ourselves treasures in heaven.

Tomorrow May Be Too Late: A sermon by D.L. Moody

Hell

A man came to me the other day and said: "I like your preaching. You don't preach hell, and I suppose you don't believe in one."

Now I don't want any one to rise up in the Judgment and say that I was not a faithful preacher of the Word of God. It is my duty to preach God's Word just as He gives it to me. I have no right to pick out a text here and there, and say, "I don't believe that." If I throw out one text I must throw out all, for in the same Bible I read of rewards and punishments, Heaven and hell. No one ever drew such a picture of hell as the Son of God. No one could do it, for He alone knew what the future would be. He didn't keep back this doctrine of retribution, but preached it out plainly; preached it, too, with pure love, just as a mother would warn her son of the end of his course of sin.

We won't need any one to condemn us at the bar of God; it will be our own conscience that will come up as a witness against us. God won't condemn us at His bar; we shall condemn ourselves. Memory is God's officer, and when He shall touch these secret springs and say, "Son, daughter, remember"—then tramp, tramp, tramp will come before us, in a long procession, all the sins we have ever committed.

I have been twice in the jaws of death. Once I was drowning and was about to sink, when I was rescued. In the twinkling of an eye everything I had said, done, or thought of flashed across my mind. I do not understand how everything in a man's life can be crowded into his recollection in an instant of time, but it all flashed through my mind at once.

Another time I was caught in the Clark Street bridge and thought I was dying. Then memory seemed to bring all my life back to me again. It is just so that all things we think we have forgotten will come back by and by. It is only a question of time. We shall hear the words, "Son, remember," and it is a good deal better to remember our sins now, and be saved from them, than to put off repentance till it is too late to do any good.

You laugh at the Bible; but how many there are in that lost world today who would give countless treasures if they had the blessed Bible there! You may make sport of Ministers, but bear in mind there will be no preaching of the Gospel there. Here they are God's messengers to you—loving friends that look after your soul. You may have some friends praying for your salvation today; but remember, you will not have one in that lost world. There will be no one to come and put his hand on your shoulder and weep over you there and invite you to come to Christ. There are some people who ridicule these meetings, but remember, there will be no meetings in hell.

A good man was one day passing a saloon as a young man was coming out, and thinking to make sport of him he called out, "Deacon, how far is it to hell?" The deacon gave no answer, but after riding a few rods he turned to look after the scoffer, and found that his horse had thrown him to the ground and broken his neck. I tell you, my friends, I would sooner give that right hand than to trifle with eternal things.

Hell: A sermon by D.L. Moody

Lost and Found

You might have had a tract presented to you. You might have turned it off. It might have been headed with our same text. That was the Son of God seeking for your soul. He has used a four-page tract—sometimes just one page—to seek to convert a man.

When I was taking my family south last summer, I heard of a man who would not go to church but would go to a theater. He was a hard case—a drinking, swearing, gambling man. He heard that a minister was going to preach in a theater, so he went. When he heard the preacher, the man was convinced that he was preaching at him. He went out swearing and stamping. He told all the people outside that he had been insulted by the minister and intended to wait for him and give him a good licking.

When the minister came out, he was seized by the collar. The man greeted him by saying, "Sir, you have insulted me!"

"I don't know you, sir," said the minister.

"Why," replied the man, "you have picked me out among all those people and told them all about me." It was the Spirit of God seeking him, and the result was that the Spirit got hold of him.

You pity men who have lost wealth; you pity men who suffered loss in the Chicago fire; you pity men who, once wealthy, are now almost starving. Such things naturally excite our sympathy. But what is all this loss of wealth to the loss of the soul? You pity men who once occupied a great position in the world and who are now reduced to beggary. But what is the loss of position in comparison to the loss of the soul? If a man loses wealth, character, reputation, he may gain it again; but oh, if he loses his soul, he can never regain it.

In my native town one afternoon a man went out to see to his stock. Seven o'clock came, and he did not return; eight o'clock came, and there was no sign of him; nine o'clock came, and still he did not come. It was a dark night. The news spread through the streets that the man must have been killed. When the news was flashed, people did not fold their arms and say they would wait till daylight to seek for him. The old and the young men saddled their horses instantly, lighted their torches, and went forth into the darkness to find the lost one. They found him in the pasture, dead. They brought him into the little village. I never saw a community so excited and so grieved. But what was that—the cutting from a man's life of say twenty years—to the loss of a soul?"

Is there a poor drunkard here tonight who wants to come? Christ can save a drunkard just as easily as I can turn my hand. He can turn that cup of liquor from you as easily as you turn to it now.

Dwight L. Moody

There was among those who came to our meetings in New York a man who came every night but never seemed to get any light, never seemed to come any nearer God. I almost got tired of speaking with him. But one night when some young men were giving their experiences, he got up. I wondered why, because the very last time I spoke to him he seemed more hopeless than ever. He got up and told how he had become a Christian. He said one day he was walking down Broadway and the street was crowded with people and carriages and horses. This thought came to him: If I only gave my consent, the Lord would save me. He said he gave it at once and he was accepted. (He was one of the most hopeless cases in the city.)

Lost and Found: A sermon by D.L. Moody

"The Way of the Master"
Evidence Bible

Prove God's existence. Answer 100 common objections to Christianity. Show the Bible's supernatural origin. This unique study Bible includes wisdom from the foremost Christian leaders of yesterday and today such as Charles Spurgeon, D.L. Moody, John Wesley, Charles Finney, George Whitefield, Billy Graham, Dr. Bill Bright, John MacArthur, and R.C. Sproul.

Complete Bible available in
- Hardback
- Leather-bound (black or burgundy)
- Paperback

New Testament, Proverbs & Pslams available in
- Paperback
- Black leather-bound pocket editon

The School of Biblical Evangelism
In this comprehensive study course, you will learn how to share our faith simply, effectively, and biblically … the way Jesus did. Discover the God-given evangelistic tools that will enable you to confidently talk about the Savior.

AVAILABLE AT FINE CHRISTIAN BOOKSTORES

More Bridge-Logos Titles
from Ray Comfort

Don't miss these other helpful publications:

The Way of the Master (Bridge-Logos)

Hell's Best Kept Secret (Whitaker House)

Spurgeon Gold (Bridge-Logos)

Whitefield Gold (Bridge-Logos)

Wesley Gold (Bridge-Logos)

The World's Greatest Preachers (Whitaker House)

The School of Biblical Evangelism textbook (Bridge-Logos Publishers)

How to Win Souls and Influence People (Bridge-Logos)

God Doesn't Believe in Atheists (Bridge-Logos)

Out of the Comfort Zone (Bridge-Logos)

A Full House of Growing Pains (Bridge-Logos)

What Did Jesus Do? (Genesis Publishing Group)

The Way of the Master for Kids (Genesis Publishing Group)

Behind the Scenes: The Way of the Master (Genesis Publishing Group)

The Way of the Master Minute: A Devotional for Busy Christians (Bridge-Logos)

How to Live Forever ... Without Being Religious (Bridge-Logos)

The Evidence Bible (Bridge-Logos)

Listen to The Way of the Master Radio daily.
See www.WayoftheMaster.com

For more information about Ray Comfort,
visit www.livingwaters.com, call 800-437-1893, or write to:
Living Waters Publications, P.O. Box 1172, Bellflower, CA 90706